TATTOO SKETCH NOTEBOOK

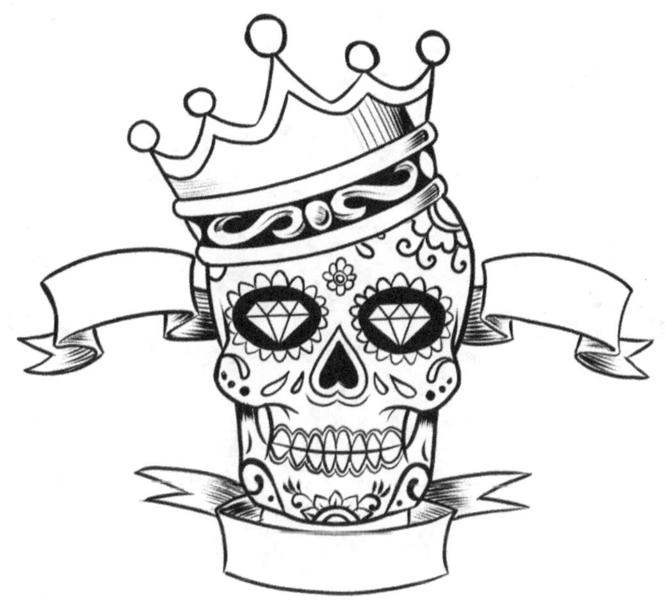

This book belongs to

Tattoo

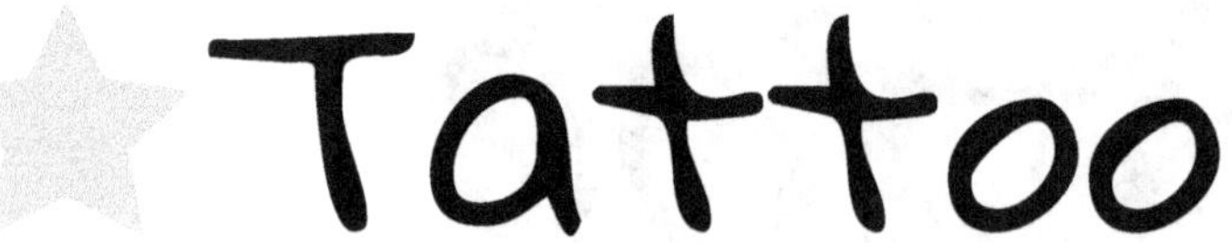

Theme ....

Placement ....

Planned Date ....

Placement

Design Palette

Suggestions

Design Idea

Detail

Notes

....

....

....

....

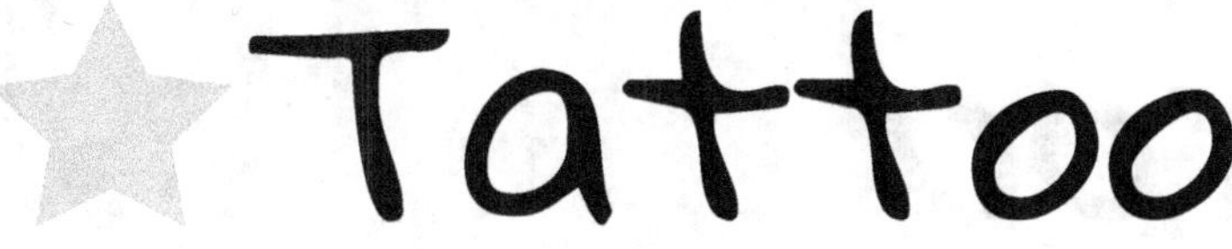 Tattoo 

Theme ....

Placement ....

Planned Date ....

Placement

Design Palette

Suggestions

Design Idea

Detail

Notes

....

....

....

....

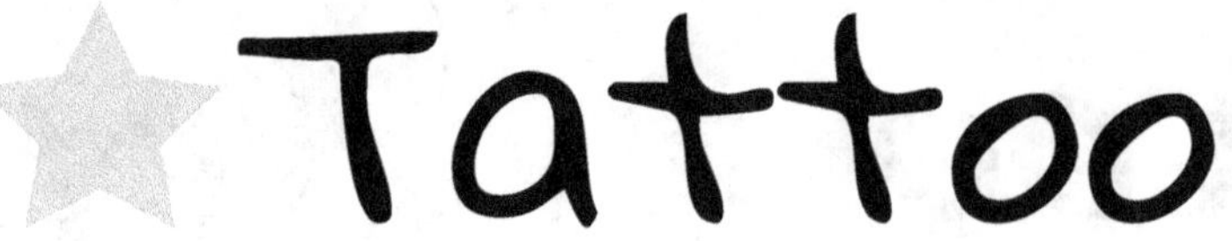 Tattoo 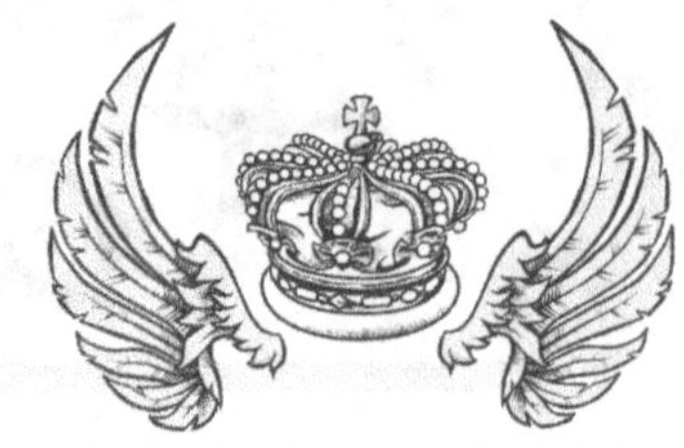

Theme ....

Placement ....

Planned Date ....

Placement

Design Palette

Suggestions

Design Idea

Detail

Notes

....

....

....

....

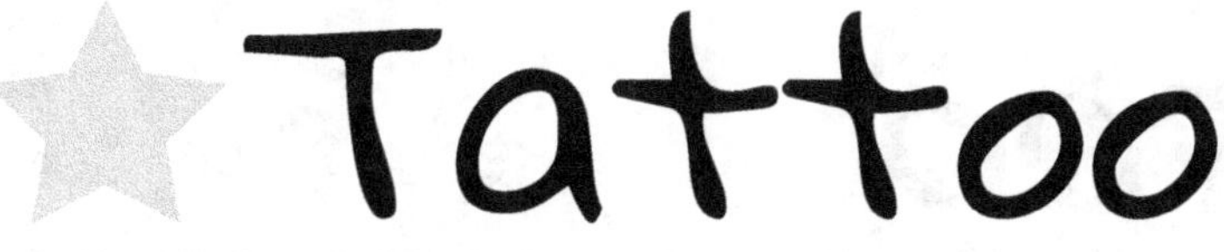 Tattoo 

Theme ....

Placement ....

Planned Date ....

Placement

Design Palette

Suggestions

Design Idea

Detail

Notes

....

....

....

....

⭐ Tattoo ⭐

Theme ....

Placement ....

Planned Date ....

Placement

Design Palette

Suggestions

Design Idea

Detail

Notes

....
....
....
....

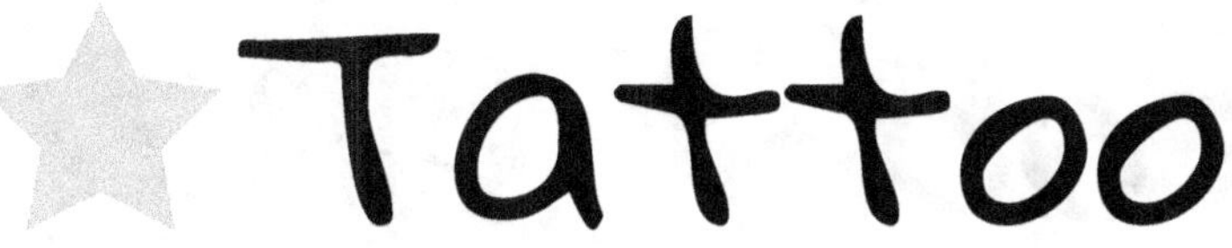 Tattoo

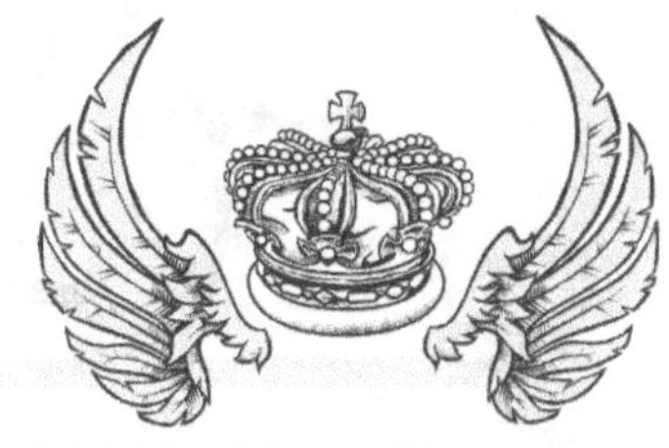

Theme ....

Placement ....

Planned Date ....

Placement

Design Palette

Suggestions

Design Idea

Detail

Notes

....

....

....

....

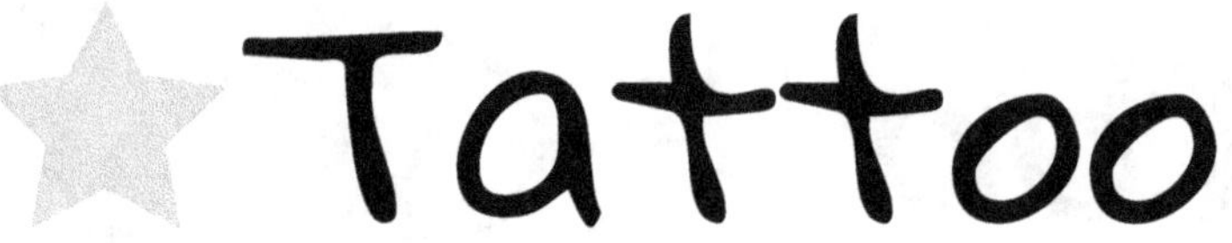 Tattoo 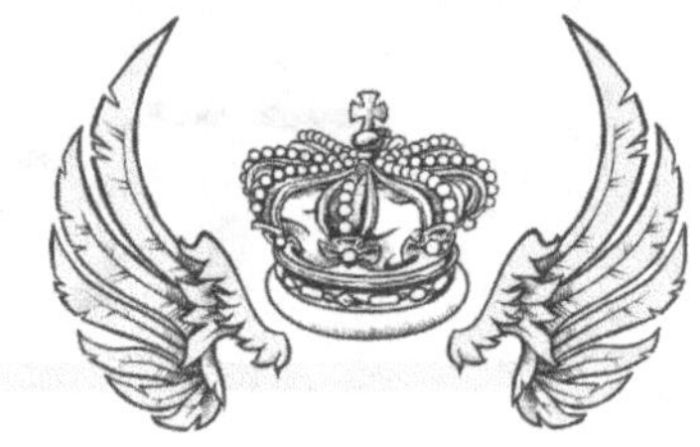

Theme ....

Placement ....

Planned Date ....

Placement

Design Palette

Suggestions

Design Idea

Detail

Notes

....

....

....

....

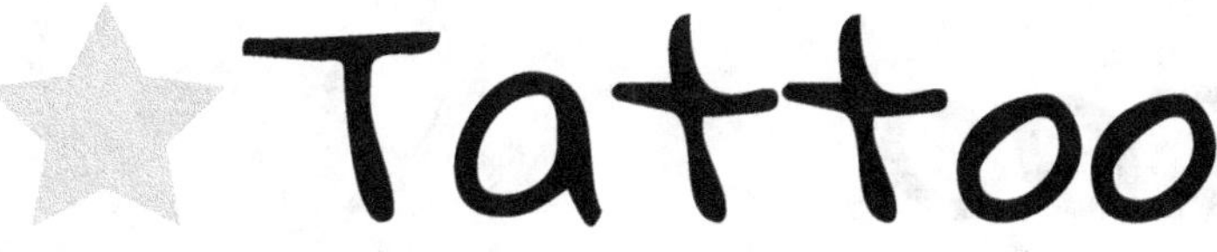 

Tattoo

Theme ....

Placement ....

Planned Date ....

Placement

Design Palette

Suggestions

Design Idea

Detail

Notes

....
....
....
....

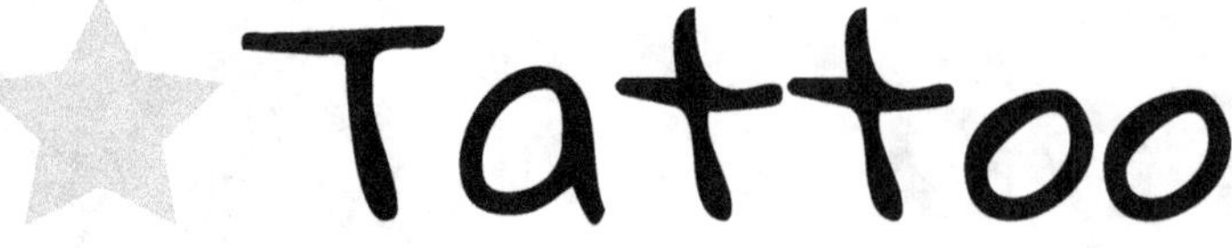 Tattoo 

Theme ....

Placement ....

Planned Date ....

Placement

Design Palette

Suggestions

Design Idea

Detail

Notes

....

....

....

....

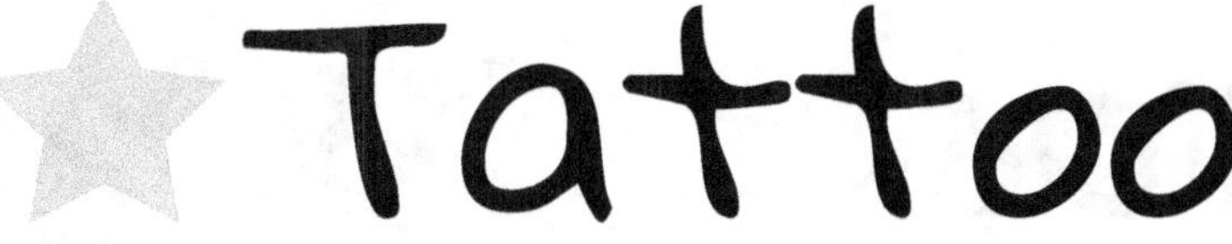 Tattoo 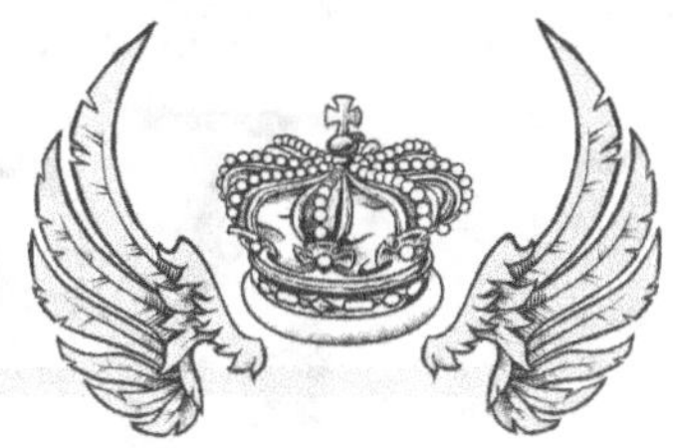

Theme ....

Placement ....

Planned Date ....

Placement

Design Palette

Suggestions

Design Idea

Detail

Notes

....

....

....

....

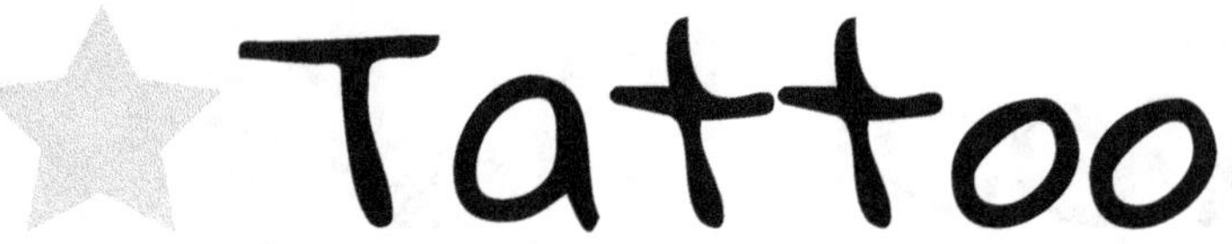 Tattoo 

Theme ....

Placement ....

Planned Date ....

Placement

Design Palette

Suggestions

Design Idea

Detail

Notes

....
....
....
....

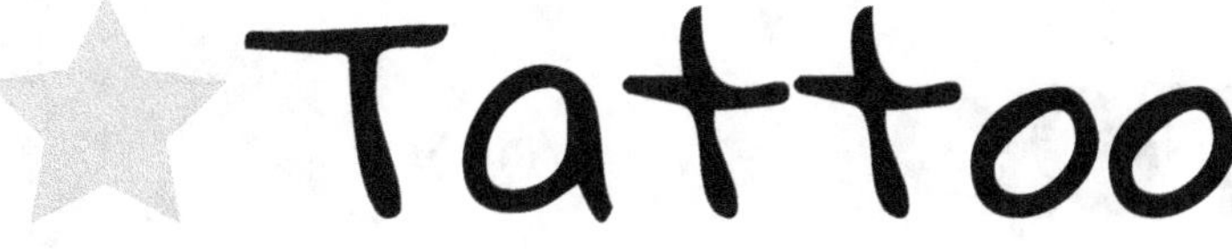 Tattoo 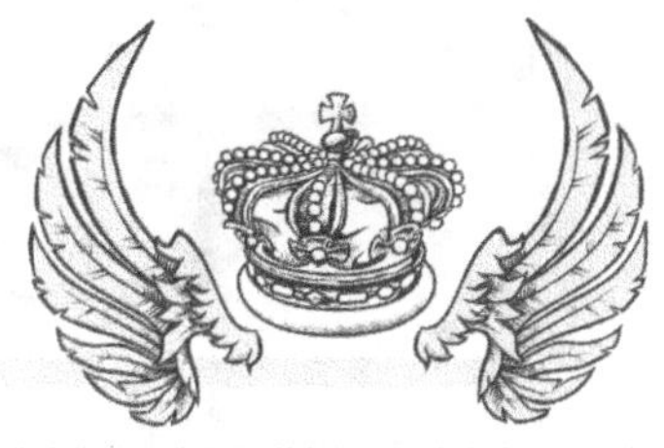

Theme ....

Placement ....

Planned Date ....

Placement

Design Palette

Suggestions

Design Idea

Detail

Notes

....

....

....

....

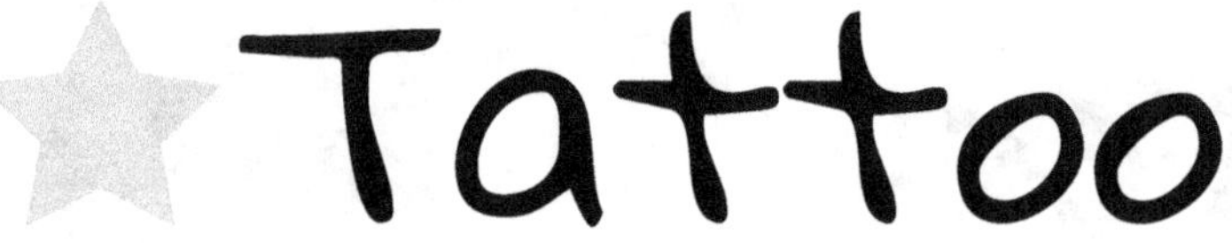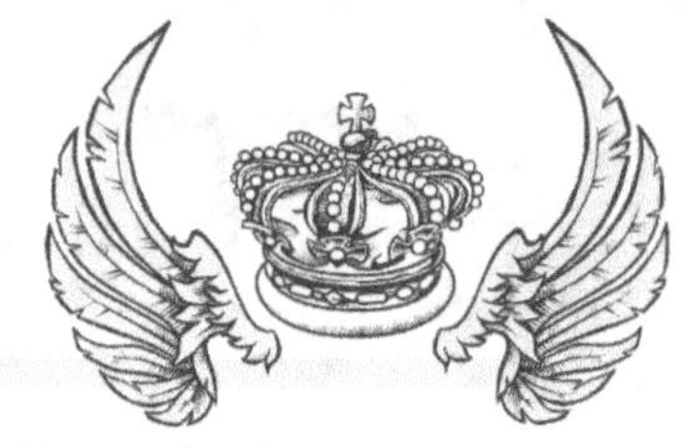

Tattoo

Theme ....

Placement ....

Planned Date ....

Placement

Design Palette

Suggestions

Design Idea

Detail

Notes

....

....

....

....

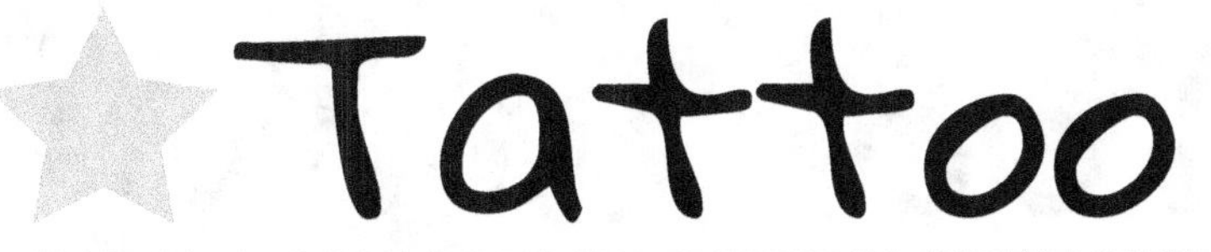 Tattoo 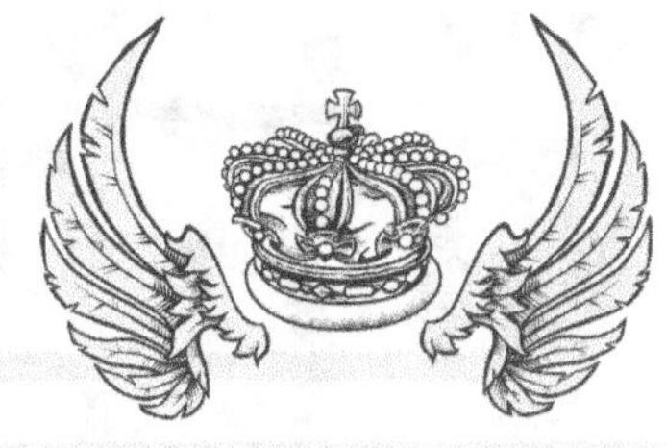

Theme ....

Placement ....

Planned Date ....

Placement

Design Palette

Suggestions

Design Idea

Detail

Notes

....

....

....

....

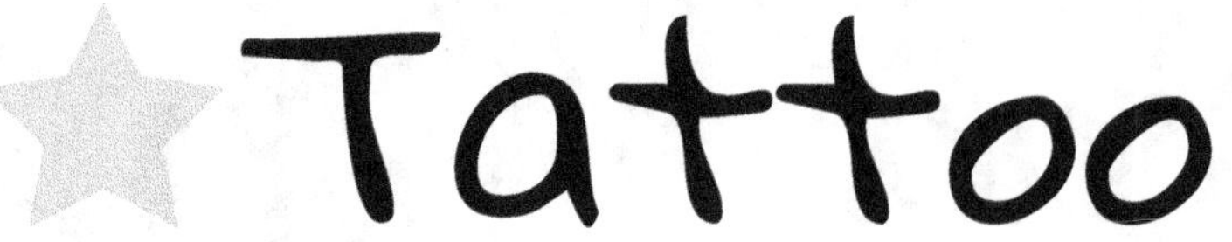 Tattoo 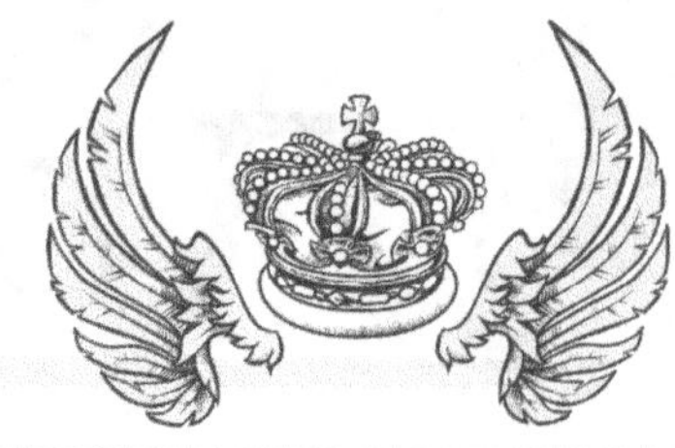

Theme ....

Placement ....

Planned Date ....

Placement

Design Palette

Suggestions

Design Idea

Detail

Notes

....

....

....

....

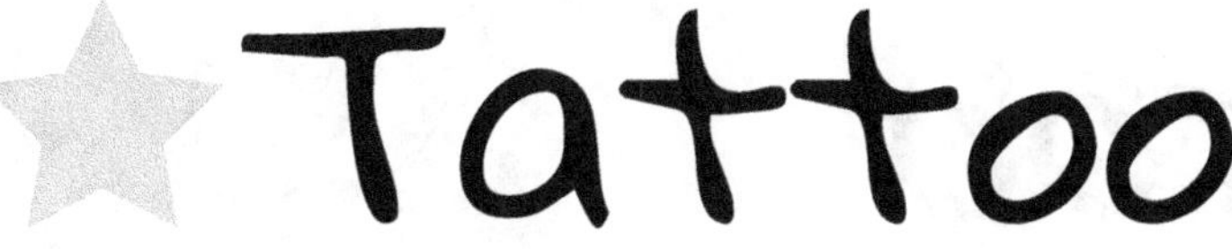 Tattoo 

Theme ....

Placement ....

Planned Date ....

Placement

Design Palette

Suggestions

Design Idea

Detail

Notes

....
....
....
....

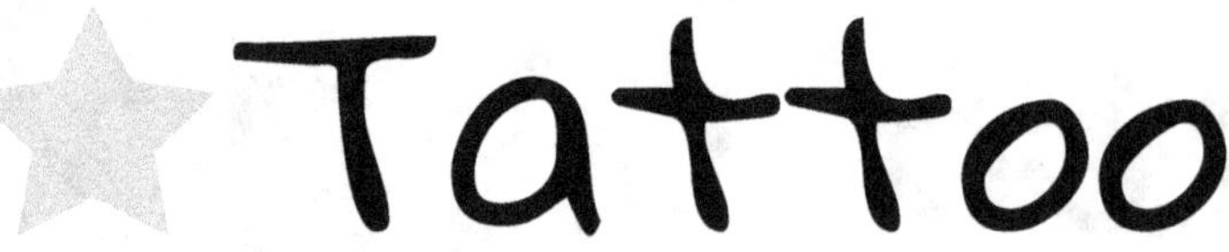 Tattoo 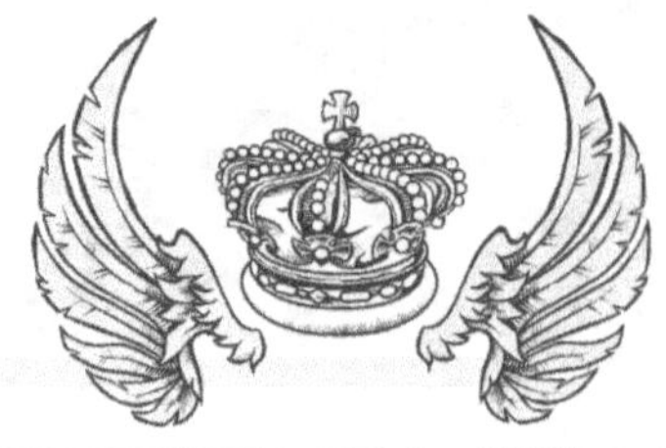

Theme ....

Placement ....

Planned Date ....

Design Palette

Placement

Suggestions

Design Idea

Detail

Notes

....
....
....
....

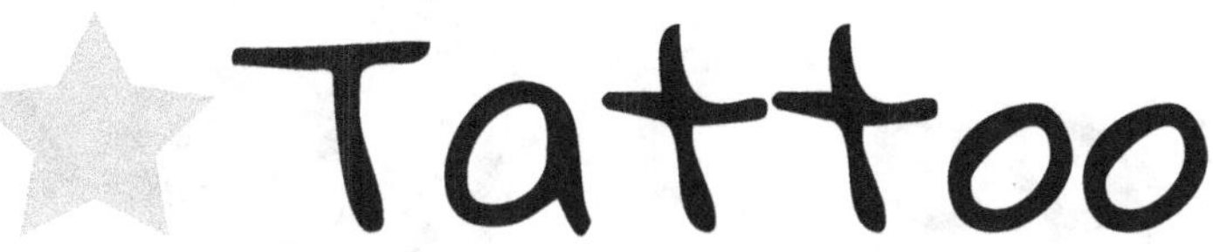 Tattoo 

Theme ....

Placement ....

Planned Date ....

Placement

Design Palette

Suggestions

Design Idea

Detail

Notes

....

....

....

....

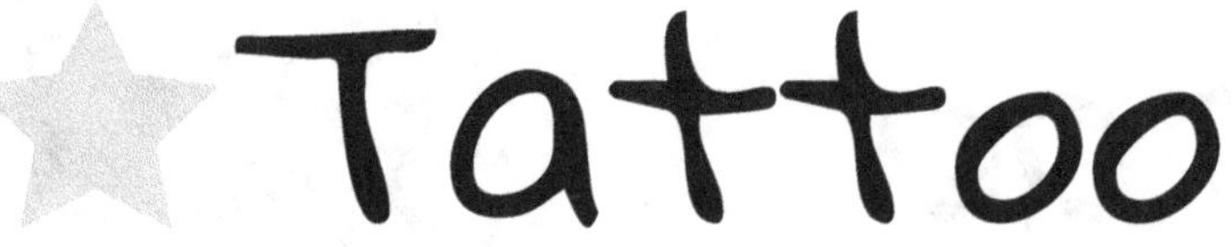 Tattoo 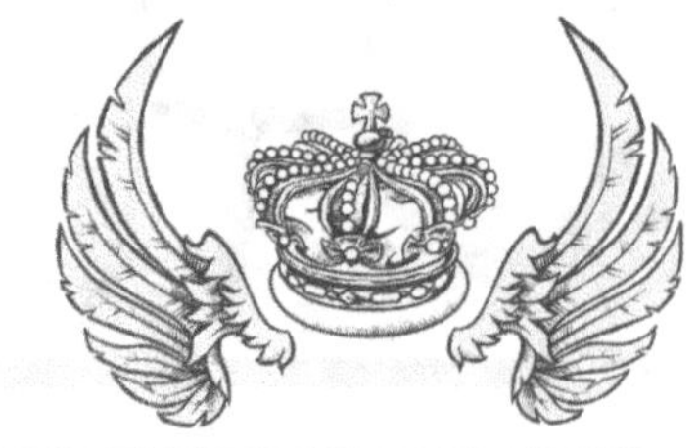

Theme ....

Placement ....

Planned Date ....

Placement

Design Palette

Suggestions

Design Idea

Detail

Notes

....

....

....

....

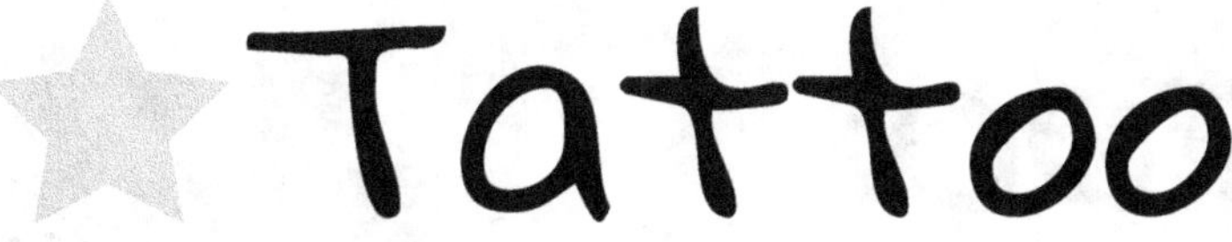 Tattoo 

Theme ....

Placement ....

Planned Date ....

Placement

Design Palette

Suggestions

Design Idea

Detail

Notes

....
....
....
....

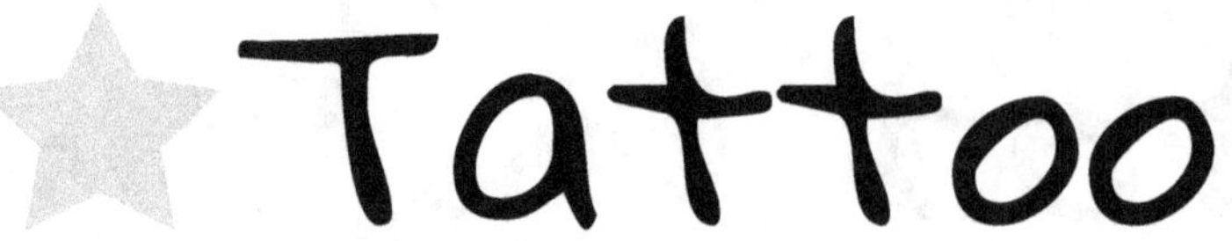 ⭐ Tattoo ⭐ 

Theme ....

Placement ....

Planned Date ....

Placement

Design Palette

Suggestions

Design Idea

Detail

Notes

....

....

....

....

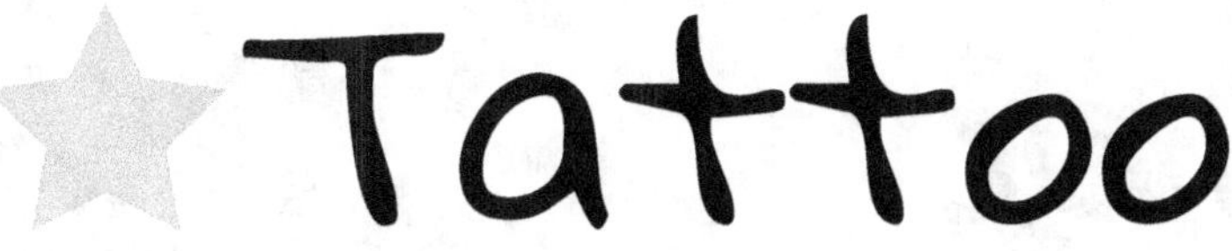 

Tattoo

Theme ....

Placement ....

Planned Date ....

Placement

Design Palette

Suggestions

Design Idea

Detail

Notes

....

....

....

....

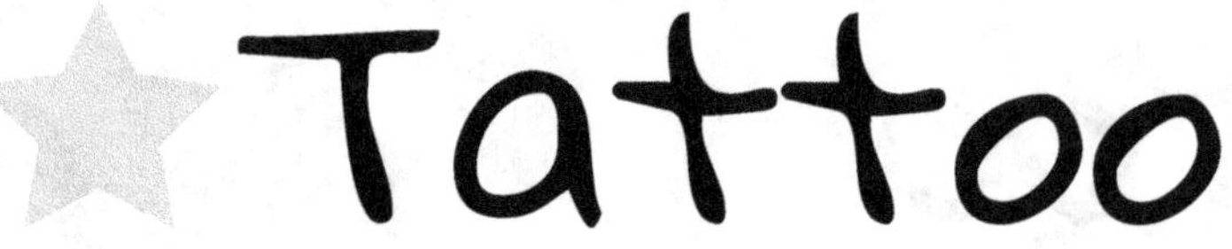 Tattoo 

Theme ....

Placement ....

Planned Date ....

Placement

Design Palette

Suggestions

Design Idea

Detail

Notes

....

....

....

....

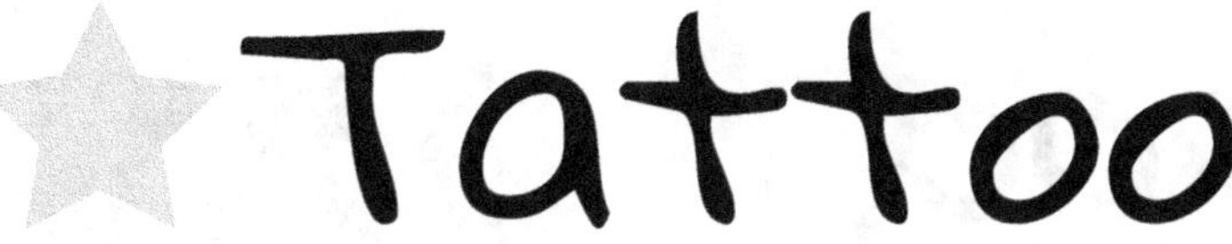 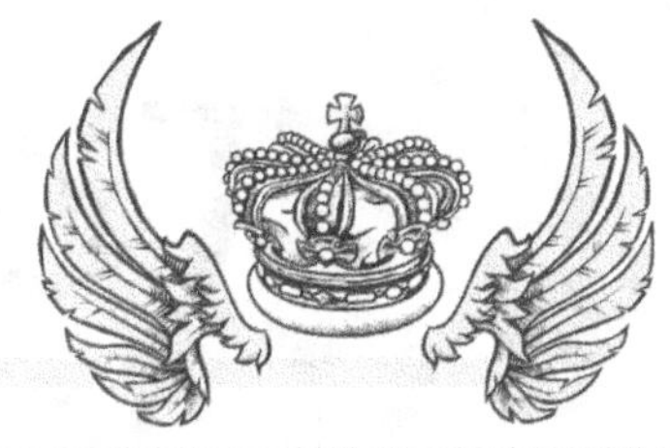

Tattoo

Theme ....

Placement ....

Planned Date ....

Placement

Design Palette

Suggestions

Design Idea

Detail

Notes

....

....

....

....

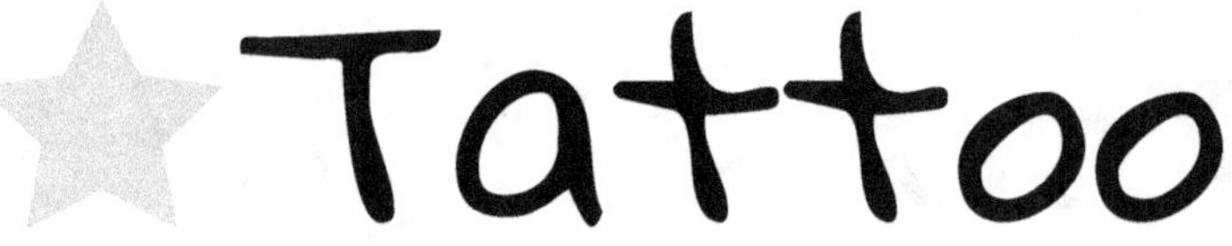 

Tattoo

Theme ....

Placement ....

Planned Date ....

Placement

Design Palette

Suggestions

Design Idea

Detail

Notes

....
....
....
....

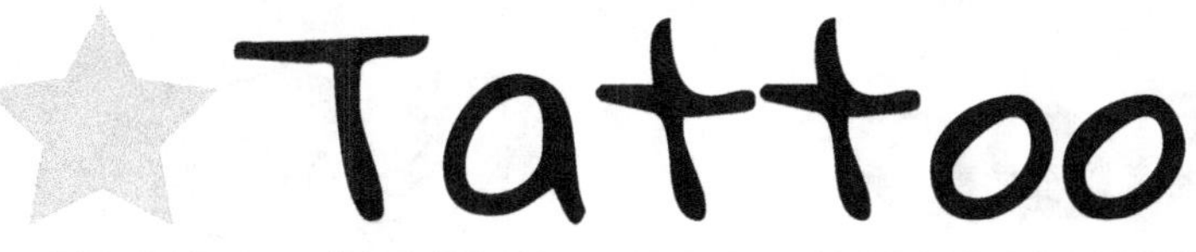 Tattoo 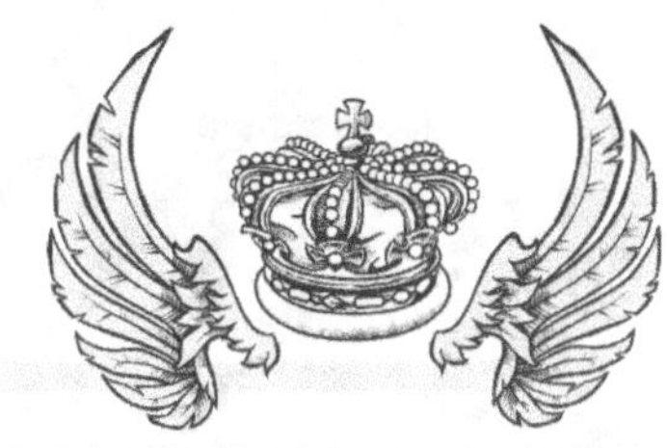

Theme ....

Placement ....

Planned Date ....

Placement

Design Palette

Suggestions

Design Idea

Detail

Notes

....

....

....

....

Tattoo

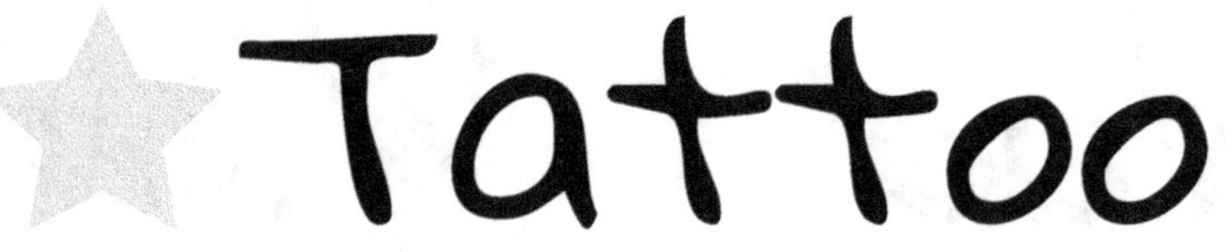

Theme ....

Placement ....

Planned Date ....

Placement

Design Palette

Suggestions

Design Idea

Detail

Notes

....
....
....
....

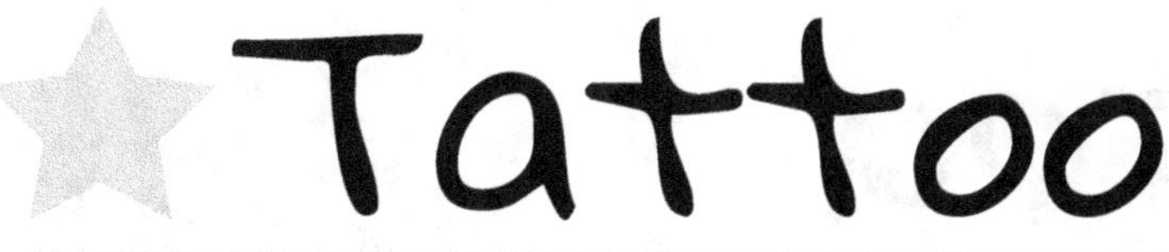 Tattoo 

Theme ....

Placement ....

Planned Date ....

Placement

Design Palette

Suggestions

Design Idea

Detail

Notes

....

....

....

....

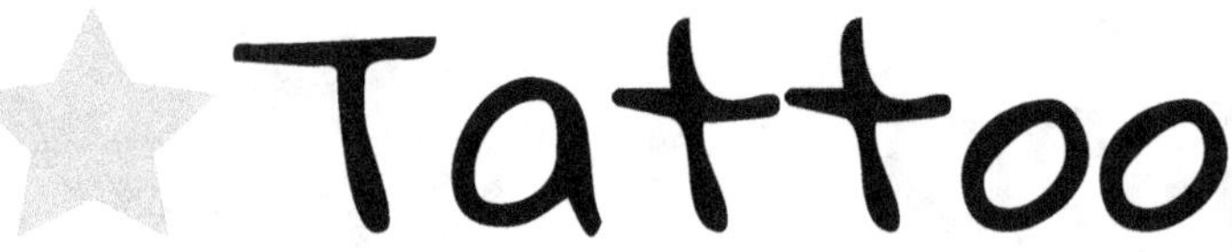 Tattoo 

Theme ....

Placement ....

Planned Date ....

Placement

Design Palette

Suggestions

Design Idea

Detail

Notes

....

....

....

....

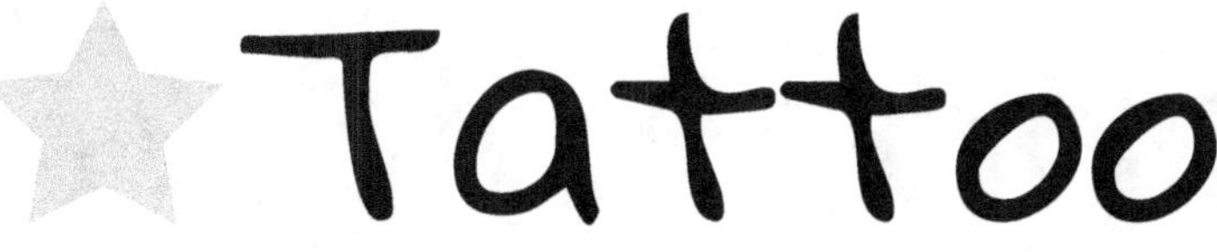 Tattoo 

Theme ....

Placement ....

Planned Date ....

Placement

Design Palette

Suggestions

Design Idea

Detail

Notes

....

....

....

....

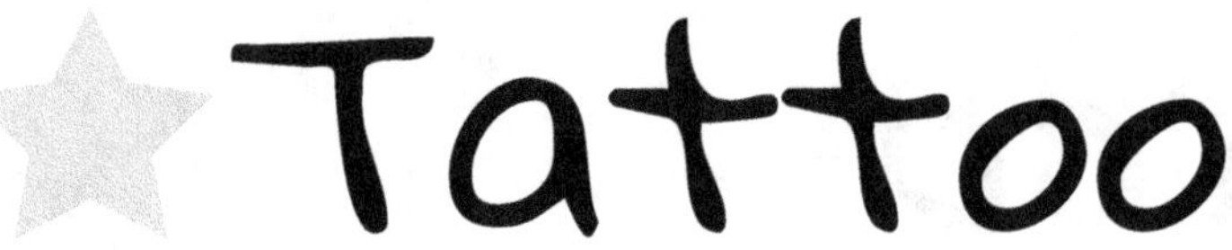 

Tattoo

Theme ....

Placement ....

Planned Date ....

Placement

Design Palette

Suggestions

Design Idea

Detail

Notes

....

....

....

....

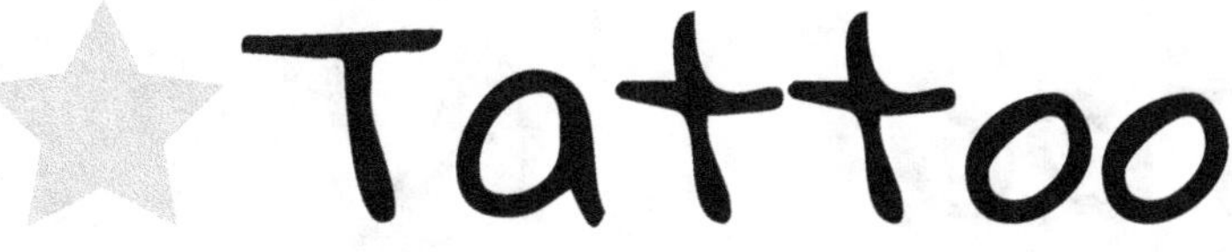 Tattoo 

Theme ....

Placement ....

Planned Date ....

Placement

Design Palette

Suggestions

Design Idea

Detail

Notes

....

....

....

....

Tattoo

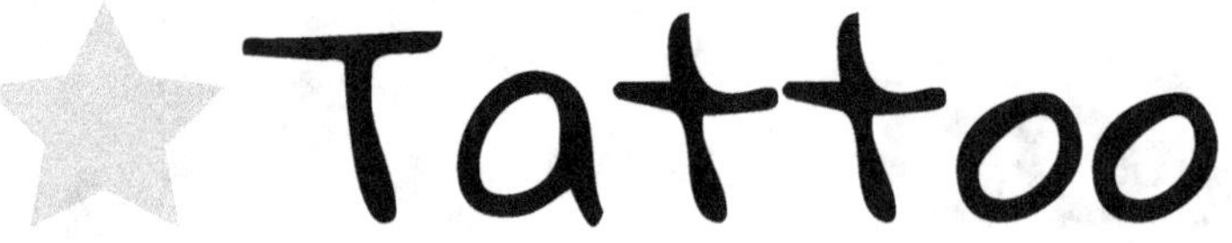

Theme ....

Placement ....

Planned Date ....

Placement

Design Palette

Suggestions

Design Idea

Detail

Notes

....
....
....
....

Tattoo

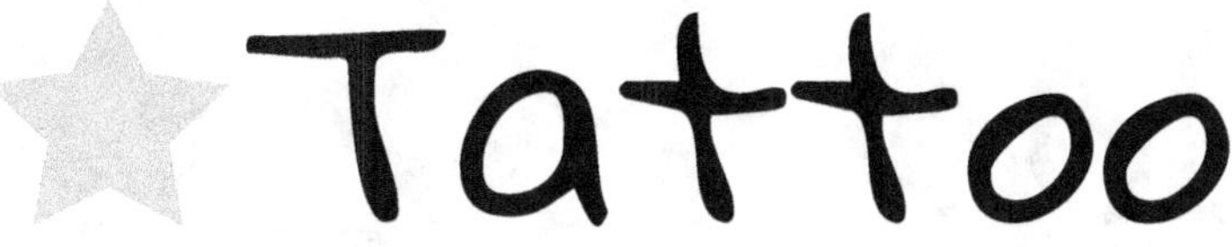

Theme ....

Placement ....

Planned Date ....

Placement

Design Palette

Suggestions

Design Idea

Detail

Notes

....

....

....

....

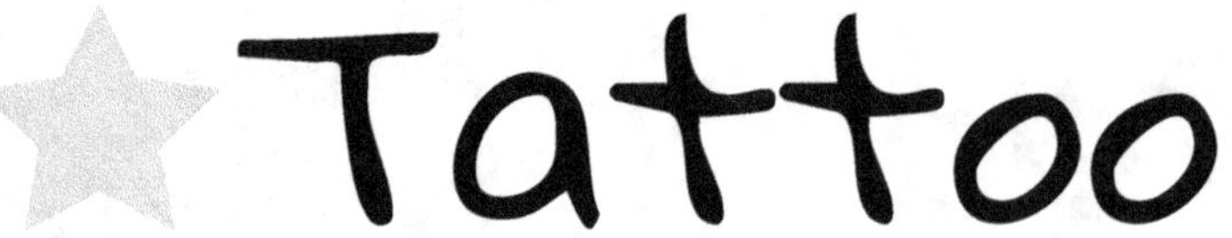 Tattoo

Theme ....

Placement ....

Planned Date ....

Placement

Design Palette

Suggestions

Design Idea

Detail

Notes

....
....
....
....

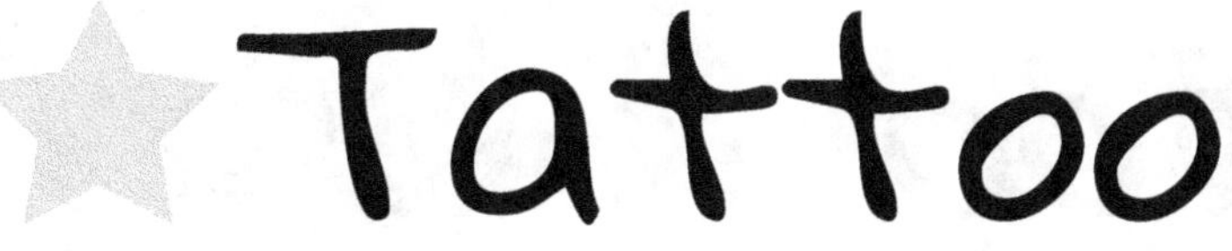 Tattoo 

Theme ....

Placement ....

Planned Date ....

Placement

Design Palette

Suggestions

Design Idea

Detail

Notes

....

....

....

....

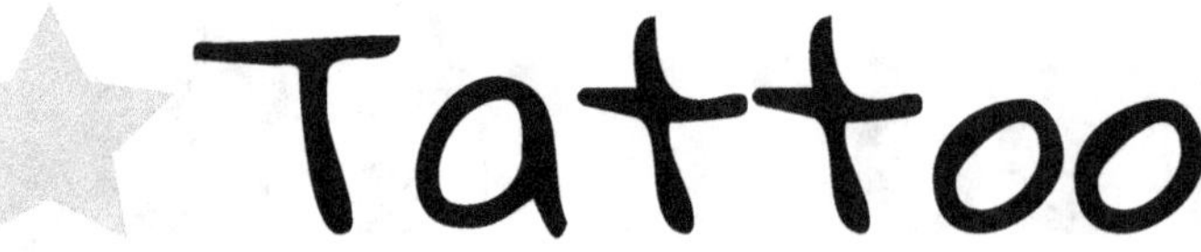 Tattoo 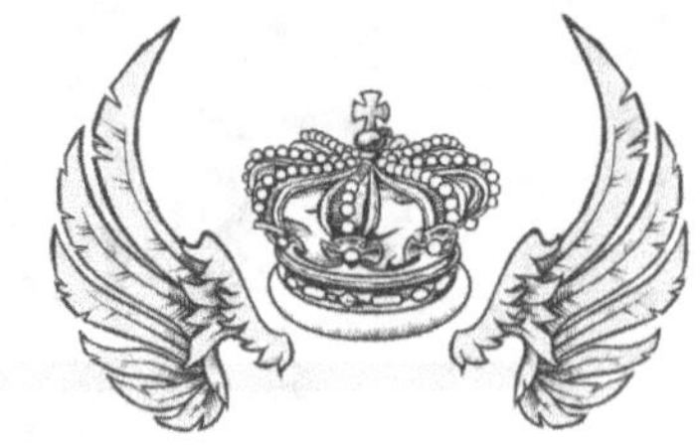

Theme ....

Placement ....

Planned Date ....

Placement

Design Palette

Suggestions

Design Idea

Detail

Notes

....

....

....

....

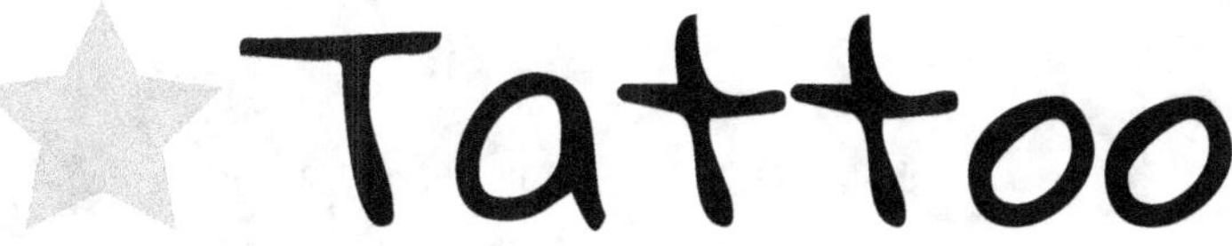 Tattoo 

Theme ....

Placement ....

Planned Date ....

Placement

Design Palette

Suggestions

Design Idea

Detail

Notes

....

....

....

....

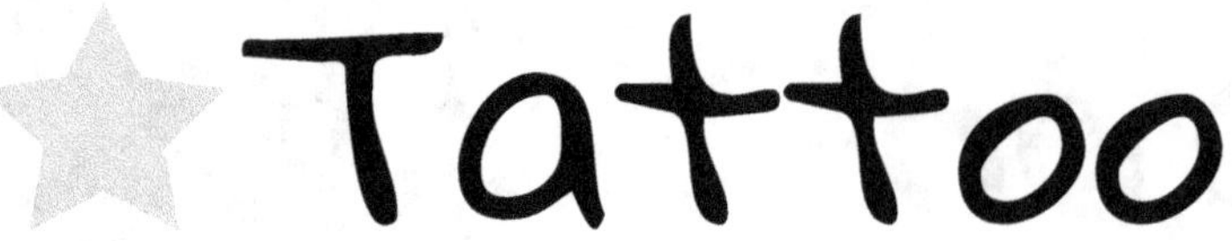 Tattoo 

Theme ....

Placement ....

Planned Date ....

Placement

Design Palette

Suggestions

Design Idea

Detail

Notes

....
....
....
....

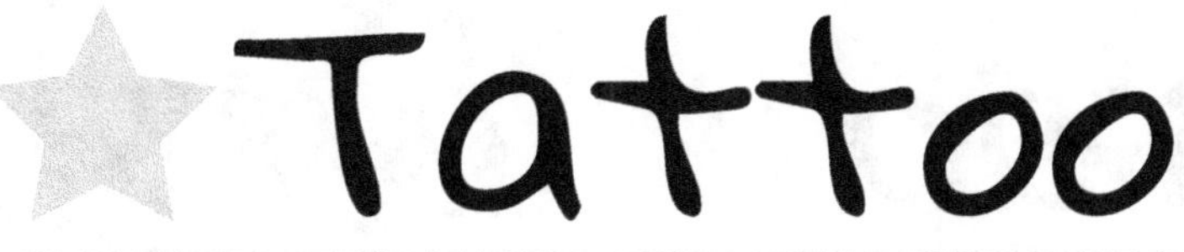 Tattoo 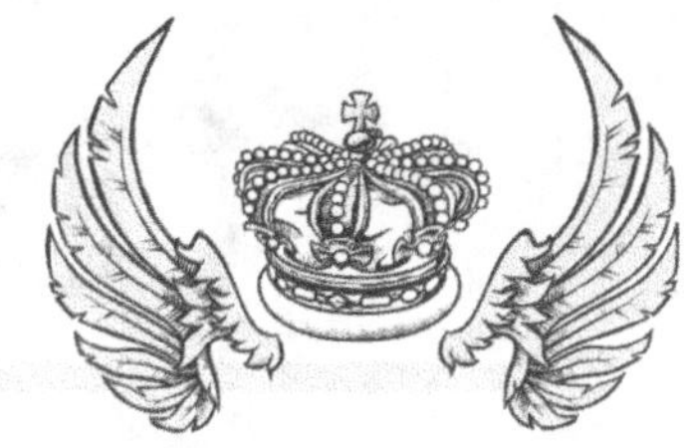

Theme ....

Placement ....

Planned Date ....

Placement

Design Palette

Suggestions

Design Idea

Detail

Notes

....

....

....

....

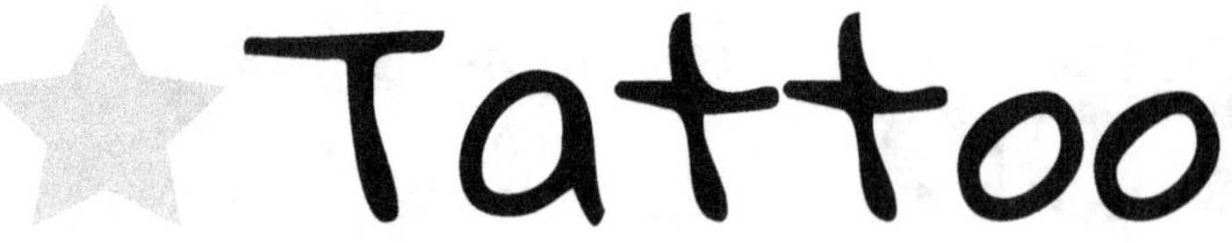 Tattoo 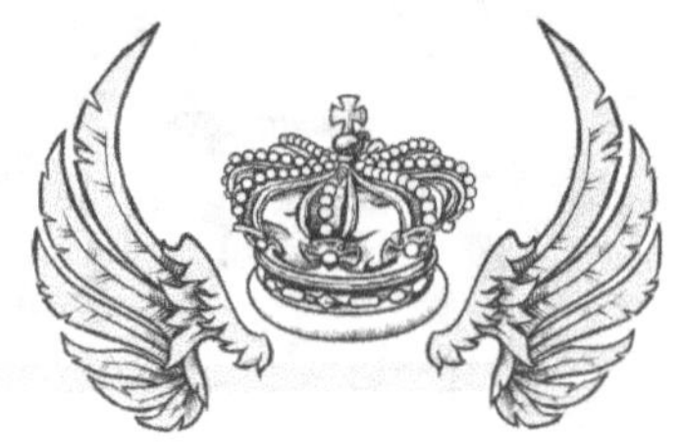

Theme ....

Placement ....

Planned Date ....

Placement

Design Palette

Suggestions

Design Idea

Detail

Notes

....

....

....

....

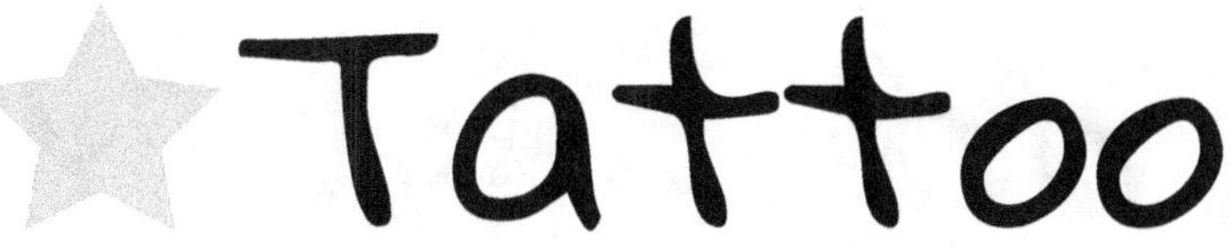 Tattoo 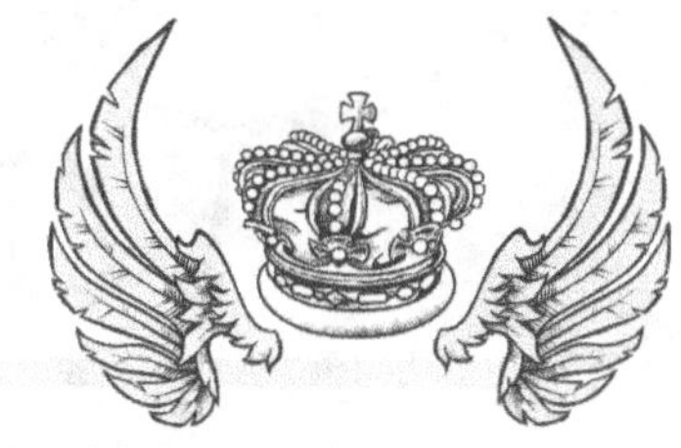

Theme ....

Placement ....

Planned Date ....

Placement

Design Palette

Suggestions

Design Idea

Detail

Notes

....

....

....

....

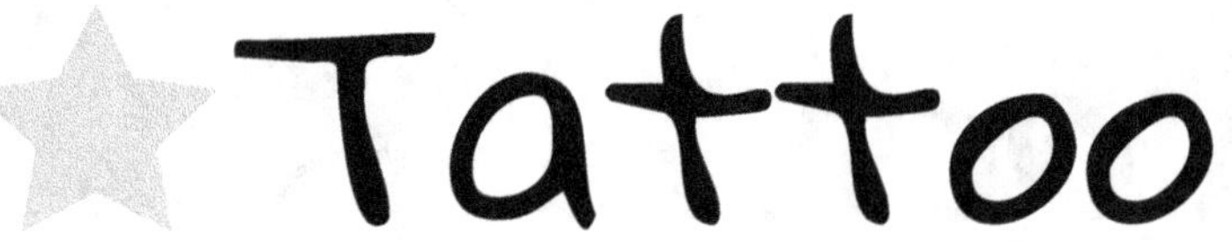 Tattoo 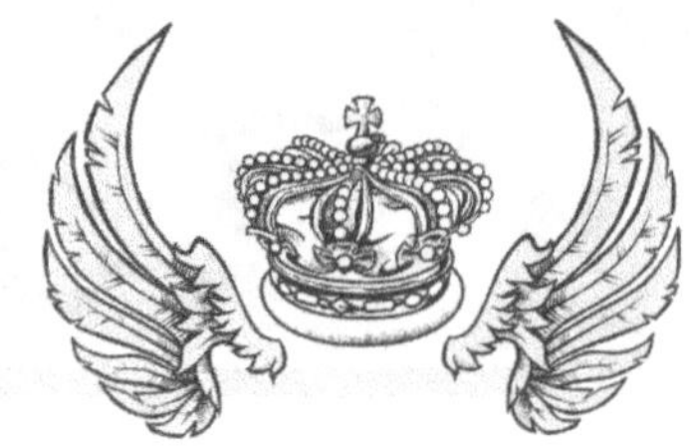

Theme ....

Placement ....

Planned Date ....

Placement

Design Palette

Suggestions

Design Idea

Detail

Notes

....
....
....
....

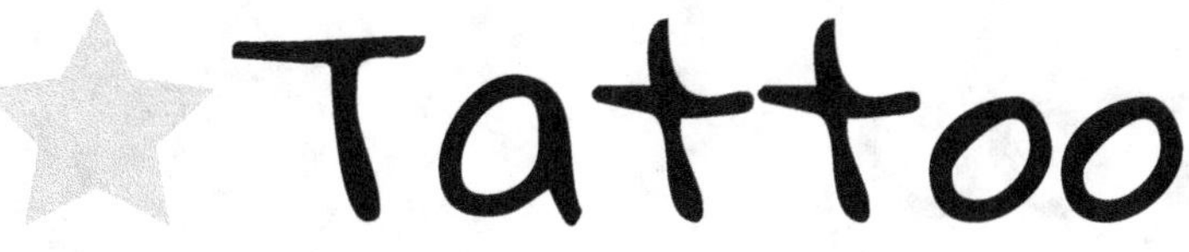 Tattoo 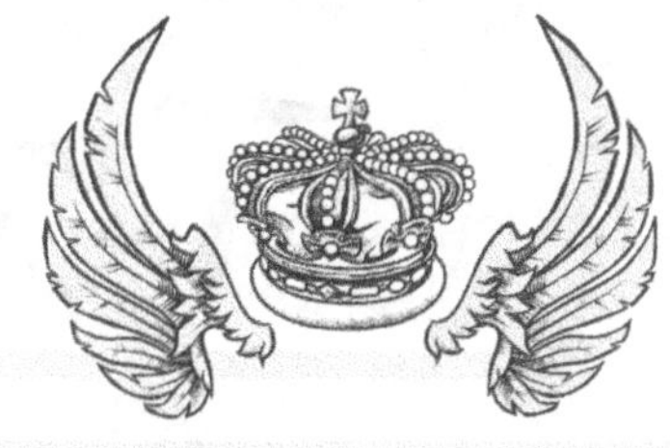

Theme ....

Placement ....

Planned Date ....

Placement

Design Palette

Suggestions

Design Idea

Detail

Notes

....

....

....

....

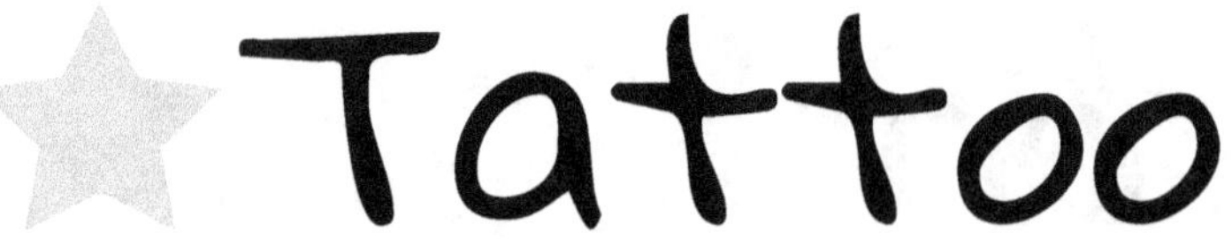 Tattoo 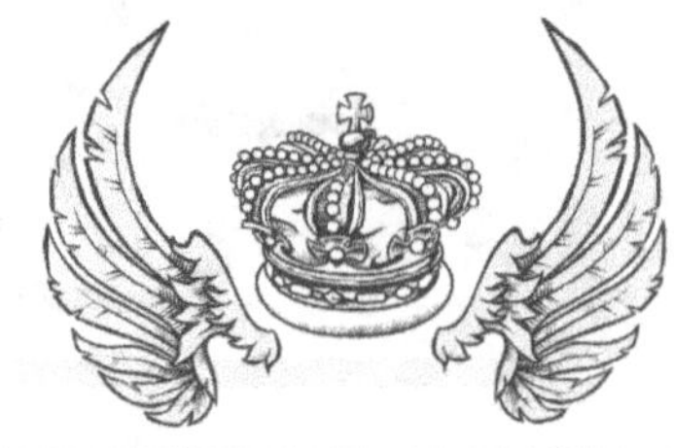

Theme ....

Placement ....

Planned Date ....

Placement

Design Palette

Suggestions

Design Idea

Detail

Notes

....

....

....

....

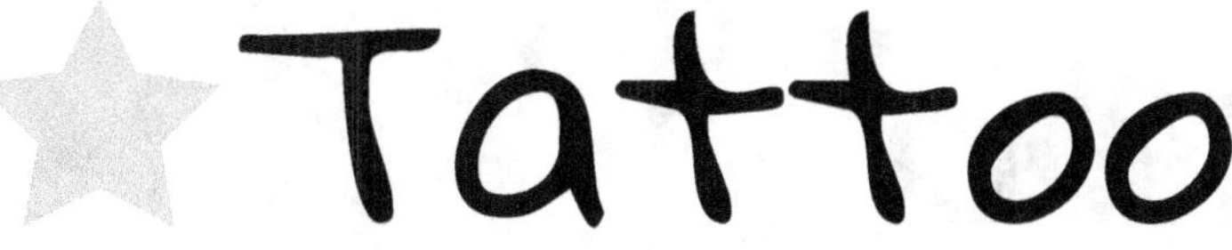 Tattoo 

Theme ....

Placement ....

Planned Date ....

Placement

Design Palette

Suggestions

Design Idea

Detail

Notes

....

....

....

....

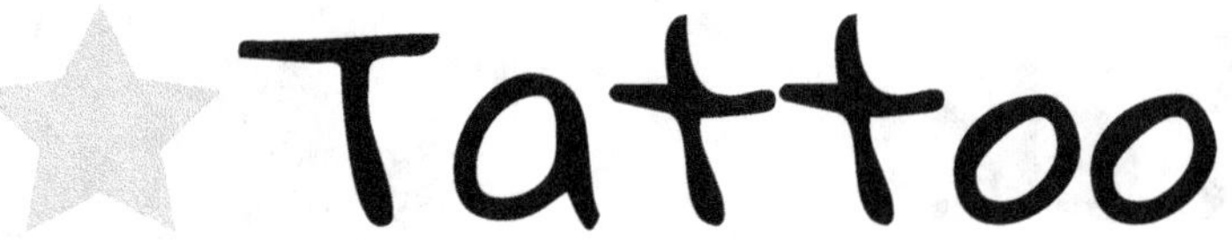 Tattoo 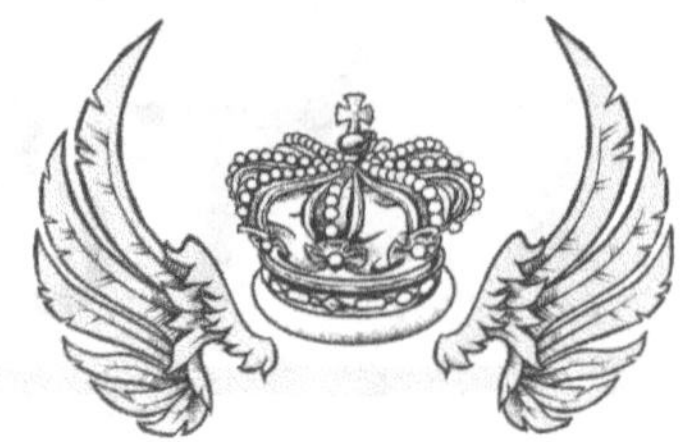

Theme ....

Placement ....

Planned Date ....

Placement

Design Palette

Suggestions

Design Idea

Detail

Notes

....

....

....

....

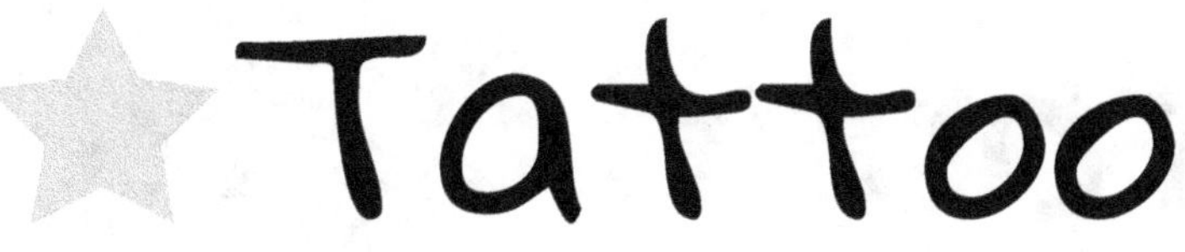 Tattoo 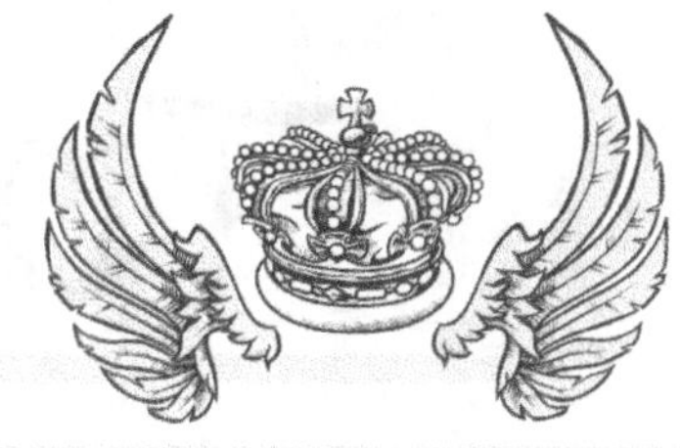

Theme ....

Placement ....

Planned Date ....

Placement

Design Palette

Suggestions

Design Idea

Detail

Notes

....

....

....

....

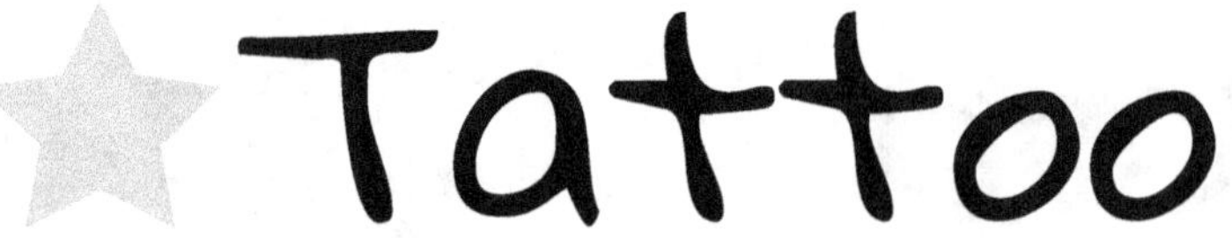 Tattoo 

Theme ....

Placement ....

Planned Date ....

Placement

Design Palette

Suggestions

Design Idea

Detail

Notes

....

....

....

....

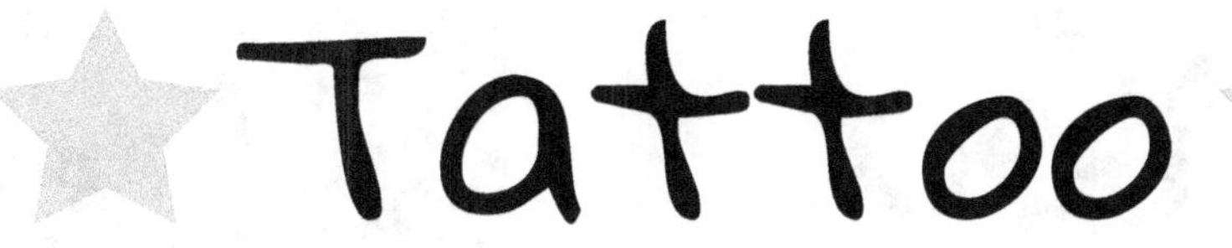 Tattoo 

Theme ....

Placement ....

Planned Date ....

Placement

Design Palette

Suggestions

Design Idea

Detail

Notes

....

....

....

....

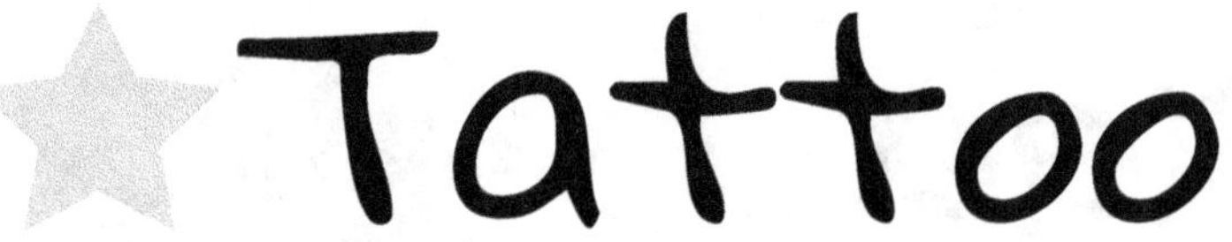 Tattoo 

Theme ....

Placement ....

Planned Date ....

Placement

Design Palette

Suggestions

Design Idea

Detail

Notes

....
....
....
....

Tattoo

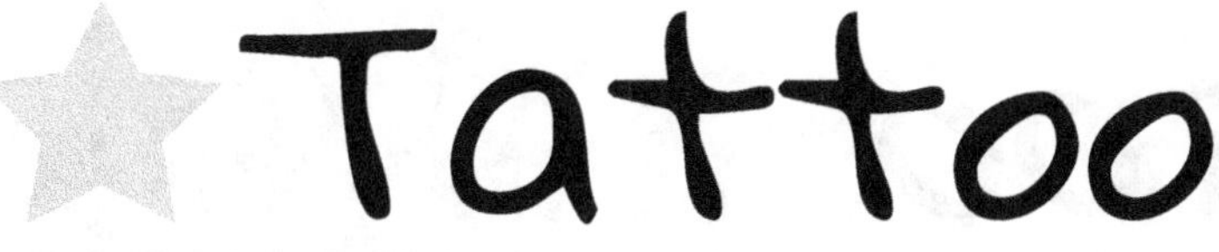

Theme ....

Placement ....

Planned Date ....

Placement

Design Palette

Suggestions

Design Idea

Detail

Notes

....
....
....
....

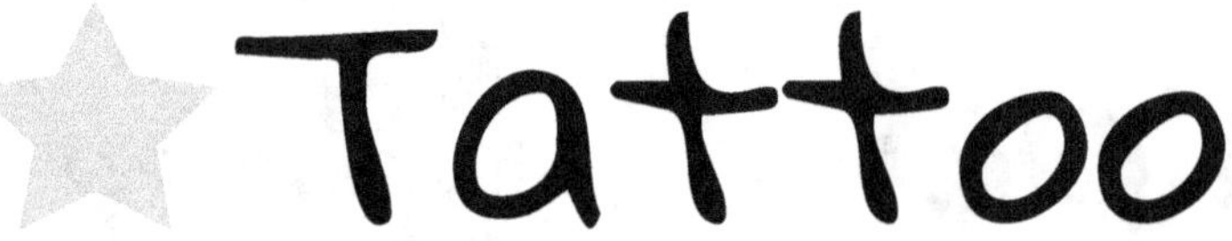 Tattoo 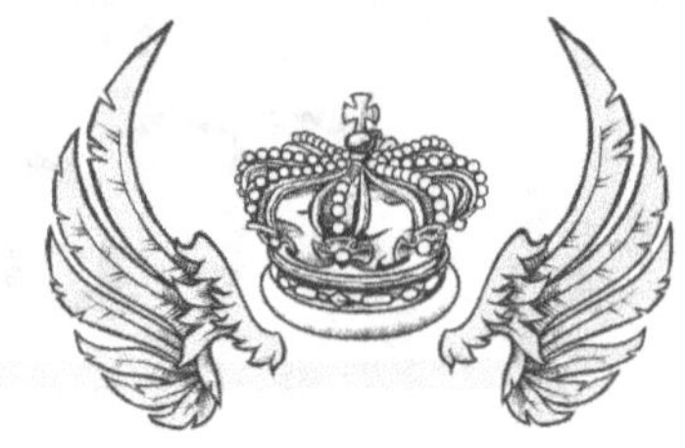

Theme ....

Placement ....

Planned Date ....

Design Palette

Placement

Suggestions

Design Idea

Detail

Notes

....

....

....

....

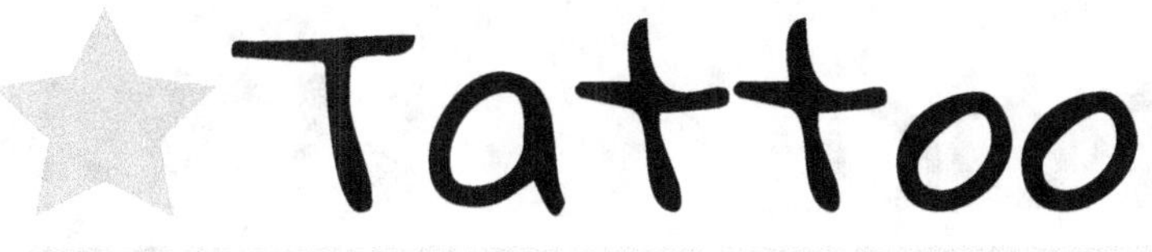 Tattoo 

Theme ....

Placement ....

Planned Date ....

Placement

Design Palette

Suggestions

Design Idea

Detail

Notes

....

....

....

....

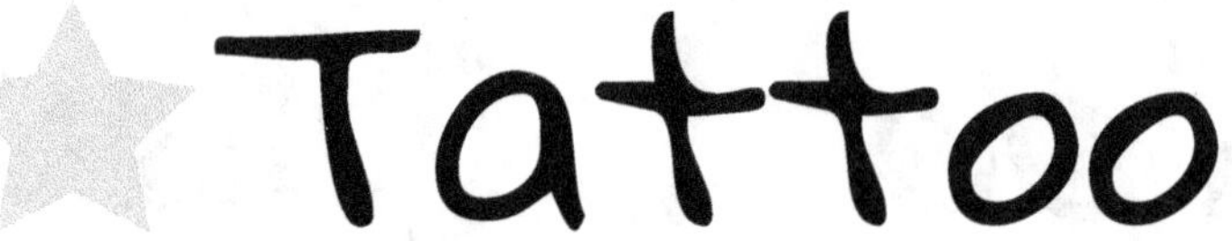 Tattoo 

Theme ....

Placement ....

Planned Date ....

Placement

Design Palette

Suggestions

Design Idea

Detail

Notes

....
....
....
....

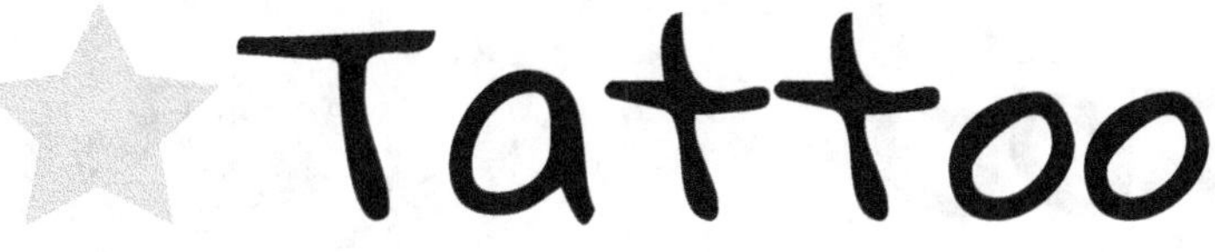 Tattoo 

Theme ....

Placement ....

Planned Date ....

Placement

Design Palette

Suggestions

Design Idea

Detail

Notes

....
....
....
....

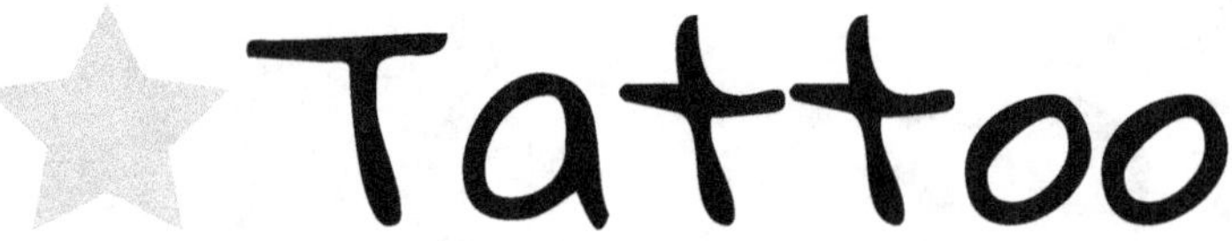 Tattoo 

Theme ....

Placement ....

Planned Date ....

Placement

Design Palette

Suggestions

Design Idea

Detail

Notes

....

....

....

....

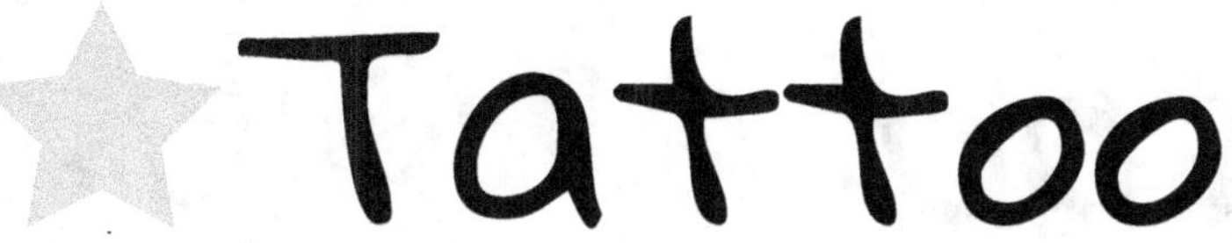 ★ Tattoo ★ 

Theme ....

Placement ....

Planned Date ....

Placement

Design Palette

Suggestions

Design Idea

Detail

Notes

....

....

....

....

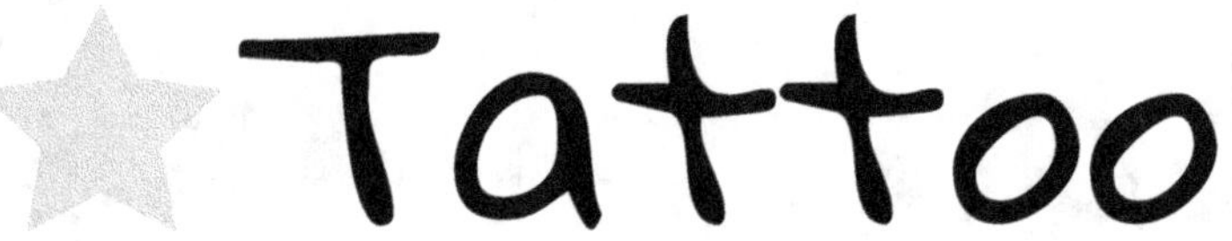 Tattoo 

Theme ....

Placement ....

Planned Date ....

Placement

Design Palette

Suggestions

Design Idea

Detail

Notes

....

....

....

....

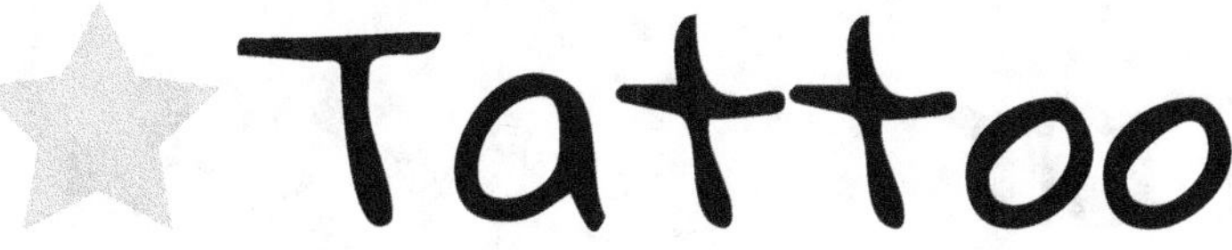 Tattoo 

Theme ....

Placement ....

Planned Date ....

Placement

Design Palette

Suggestions

Design Idea

Detail

Notes

....

....

....

....

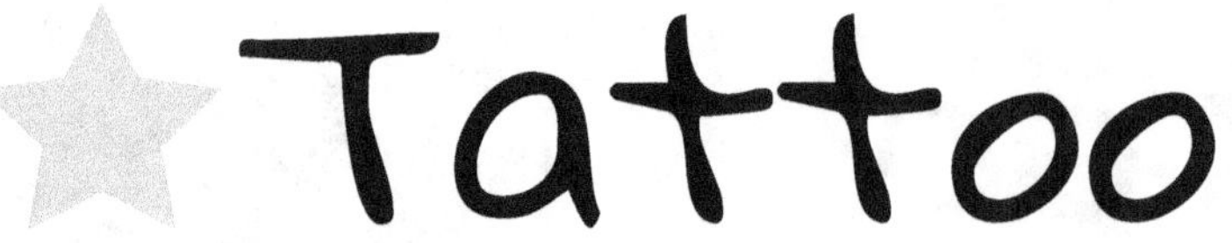 Tattoo 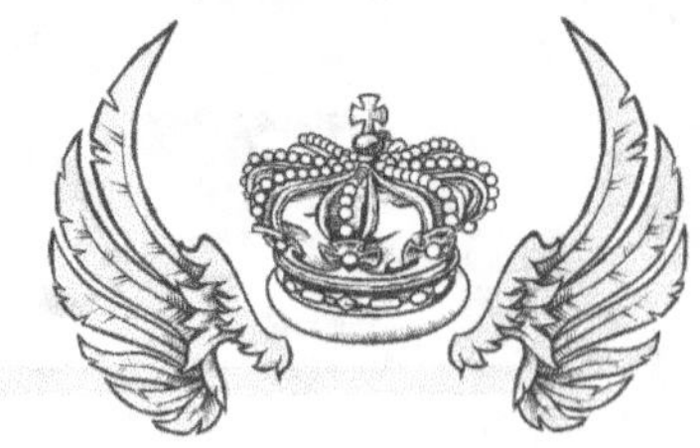

Theme ....

Placement ....

Planned Date ....

Placement

Design Palette

Suggestions

Design Idea

Detail

Notes

....

....

....

....

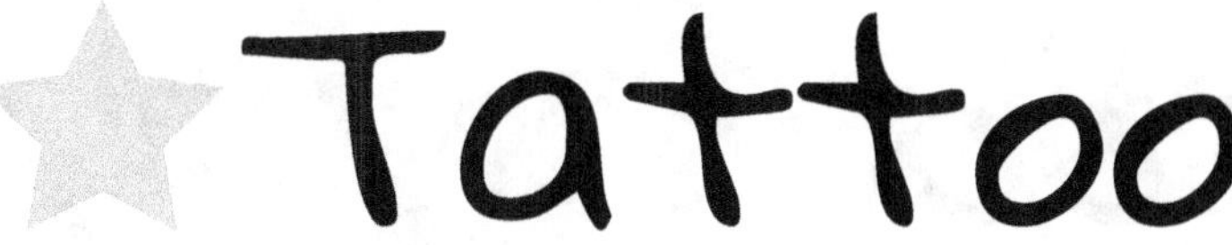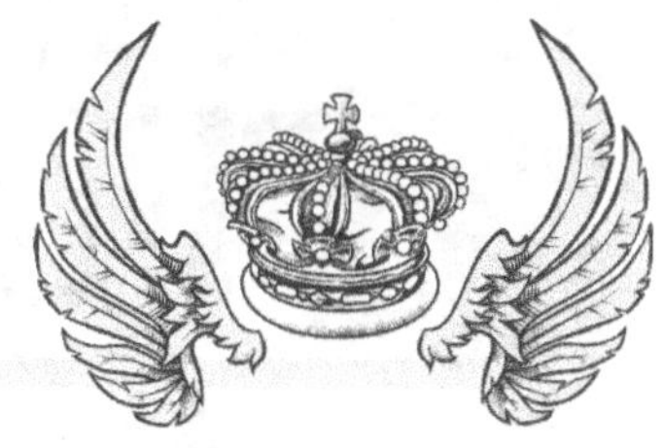

Tattoo

Theme ....

Placement ....

Planned Date ....

Placement

Design Palette

Suggestions

Design Idea

Detail

Notes

....

....

....

....

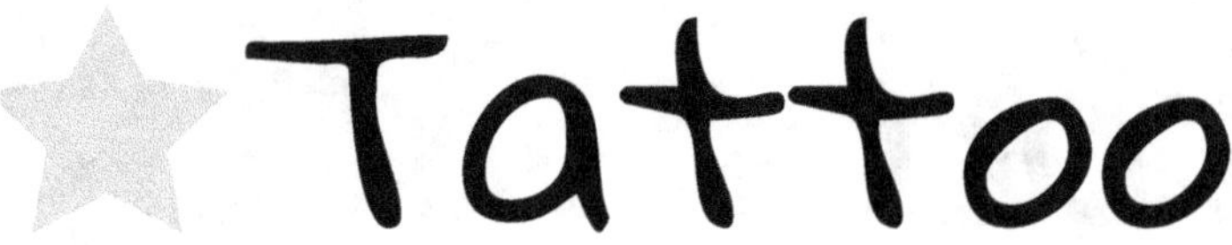 Tattoo 

Theme ....

Placement ....

Planned Date ....

Placement

Design Palette

Suggestions

Design Idea

Detail

Notes

....

....

....

....

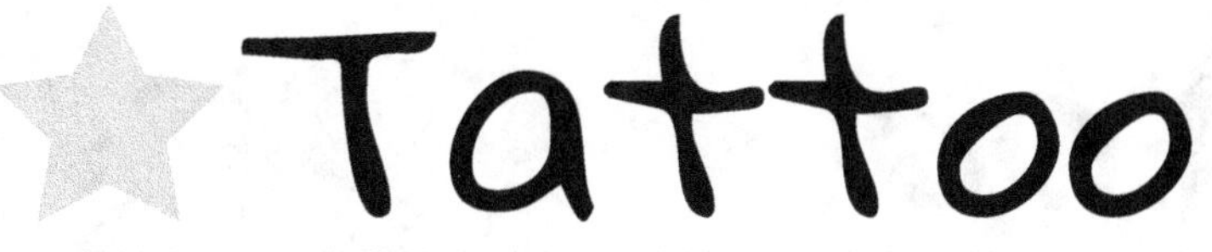 Tattoo 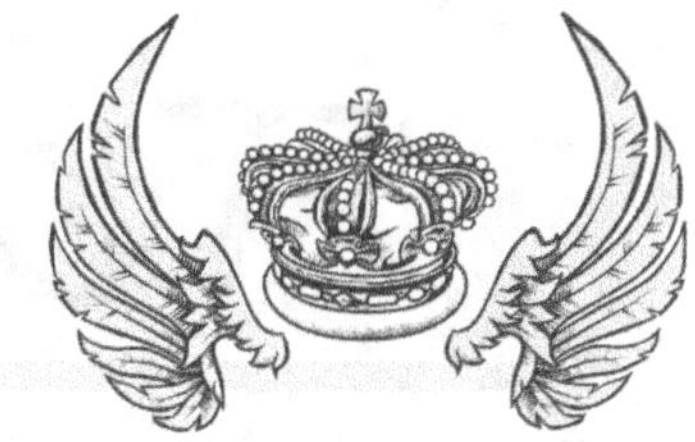

Theme ....

Placement ....

Planned Date ....

Placement

Design Palette

Suggestions

Design Idea

Detail

Notes

....

....

....

....

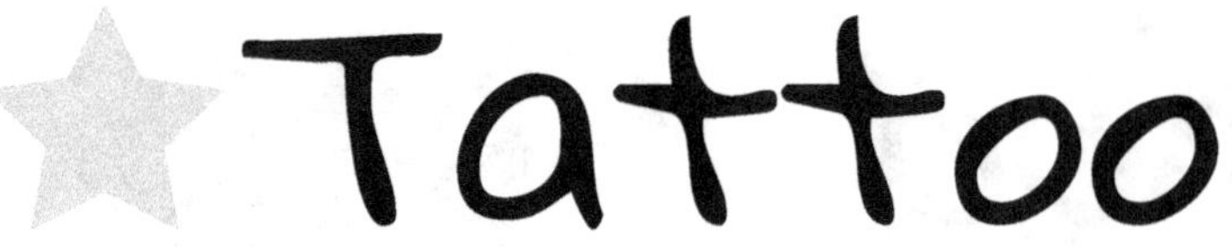 Tattoo 

Theme ....

Placement ....

Planned Date ....

Placement

Design Palette

Suggestions

Design Idea

Detail

Notes

....

....

....

....

Tattoo

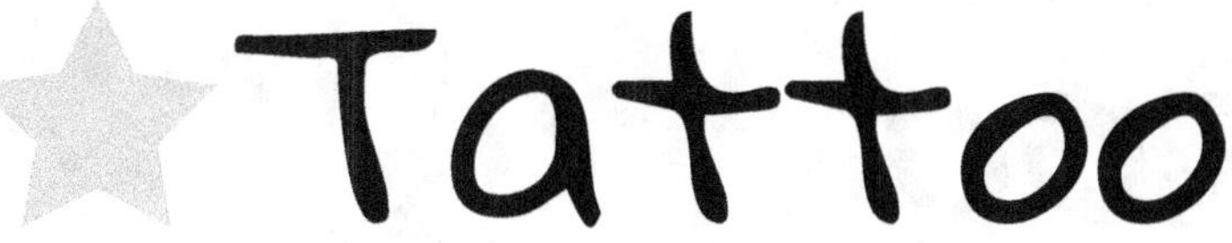 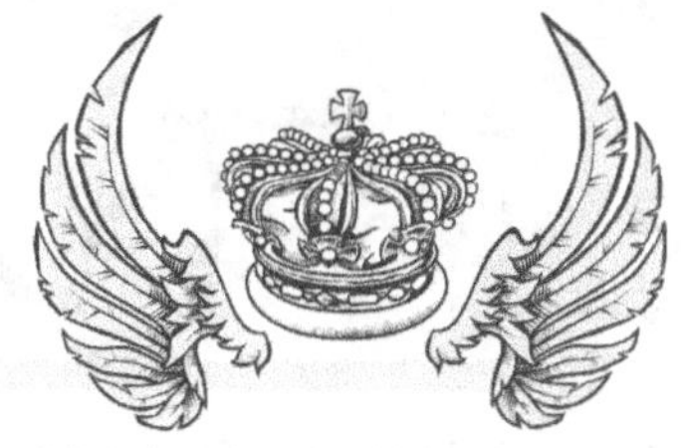

Theme ....

Placement ....

Planned Date ....

Placement

Design Palette

Suggestions

Design Idea

Detail

Notes

....
....
....
....

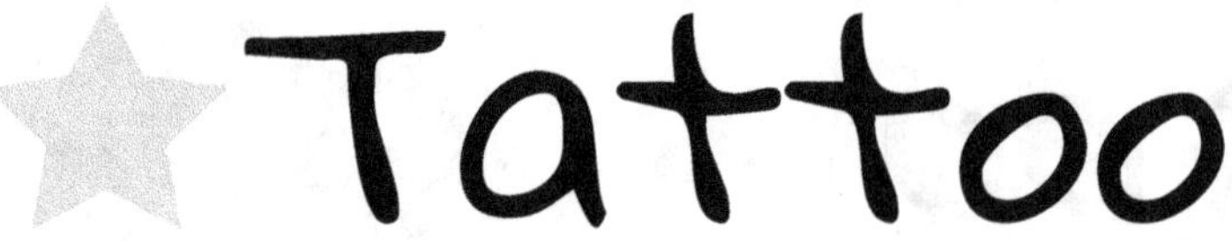 Tattoo 

Theme ....

Placement ....

Planned Date ....

Placement

Design Palette

Suggestions

Design Idea

Detail

Notes

....

....

....

....

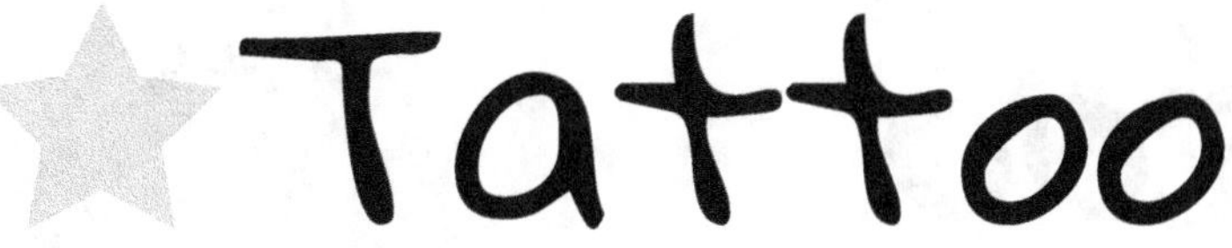 Tattoo 

Theme ....

Placement ....

Planned Date ....

Placement

Design Palette

Suggestions

Design Idea

Detail

Notes

....

....

....

....

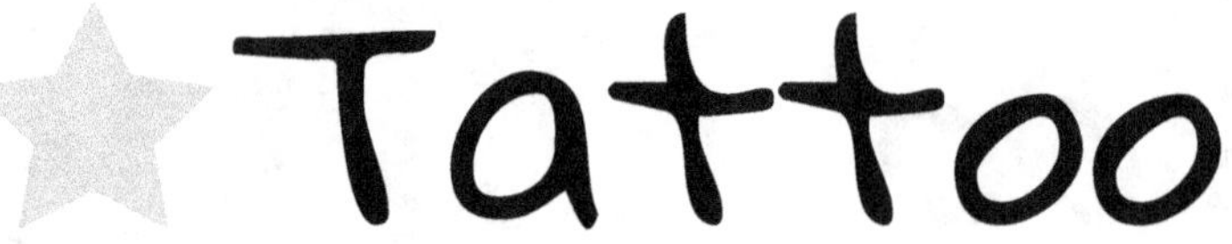 Tattoo 

Theme ....

Placement ....

Planned Date ....

Placement

Design Palette

Suggestions

Design Idea

Detail

Notes

....

....

....

....

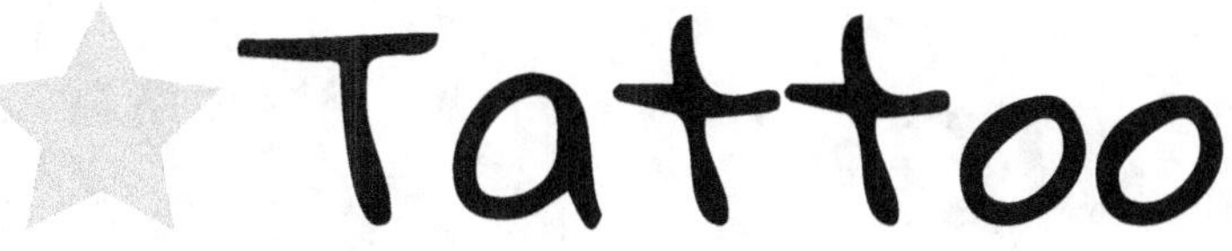 Tattoo 

Theme ....

Placement ....

Planned Date ....

Placement

Design Palette

Suggestions

Design Idea

Detail

Notes

....

....

....

....

Tattoo

Theme ....

Placement ....

Planned Date ....

Placement

Design Palette

Suggestions

Design Idea

Detail

Notes

....

....

....

....

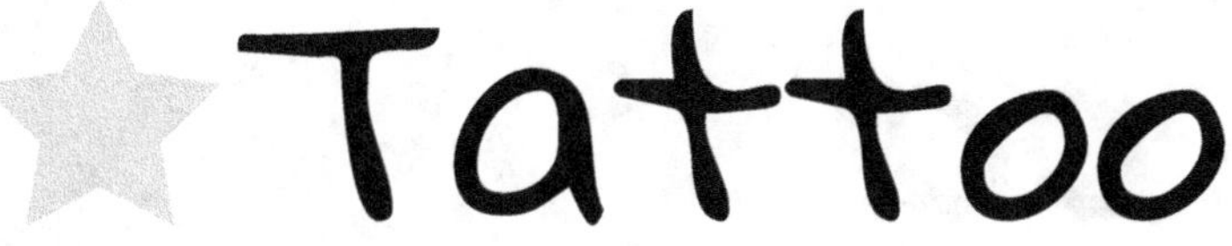 Tattoo 

Theme ....

Placement ....

Planned Date ....

Placement

Design Palette

Suggestions

Design Idea

Detail

Notes

....

....

....

....

Tattoo

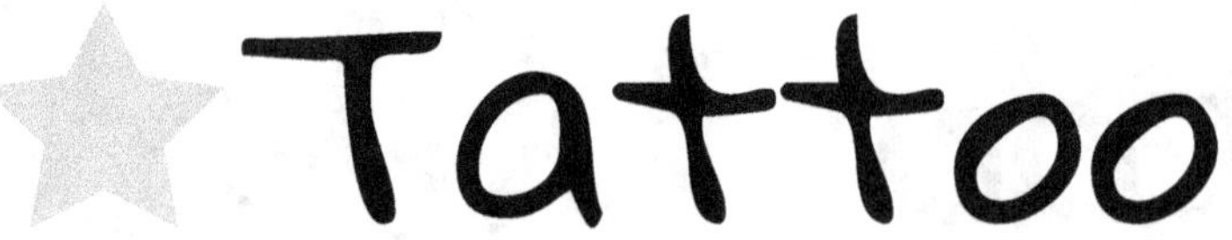

Theme ....

Placement ....

Planned Date ....

Placement

Design Palette

Suggestions

Design Idea

Detail

Notes

....

....

....

....

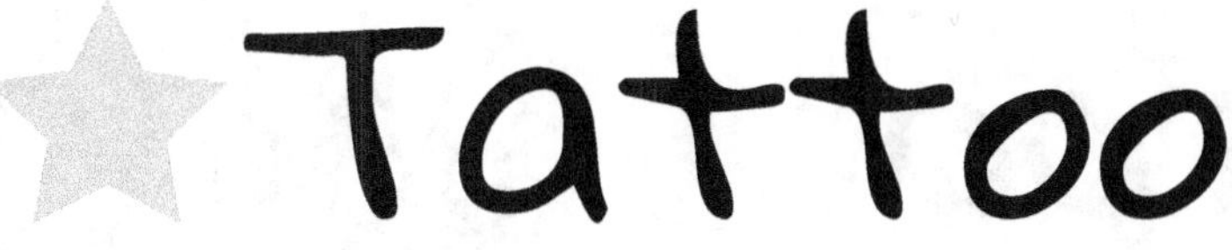 Tattoo 

Theme ....

Placement ....

Planned Date ....

Placement

Design Palette

Suggestions

Design Idea

Detail

Notes

....

....

....

....

Tattoo
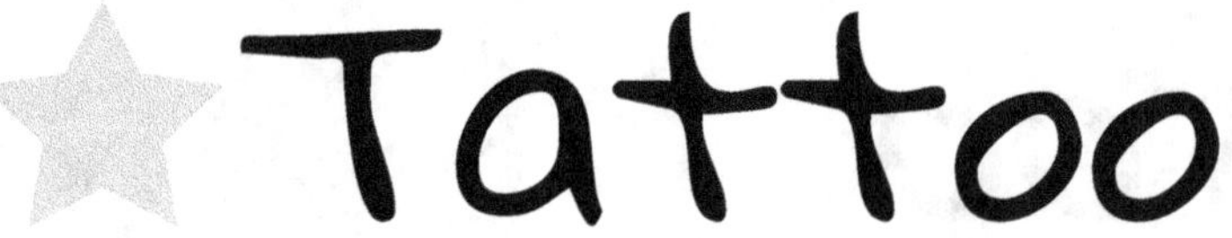

Theme ....

Placement ....

Planned Date ....

Placement

Design Palette

Suggestions

Design Idea

Detail

Notes

....

....

....

....

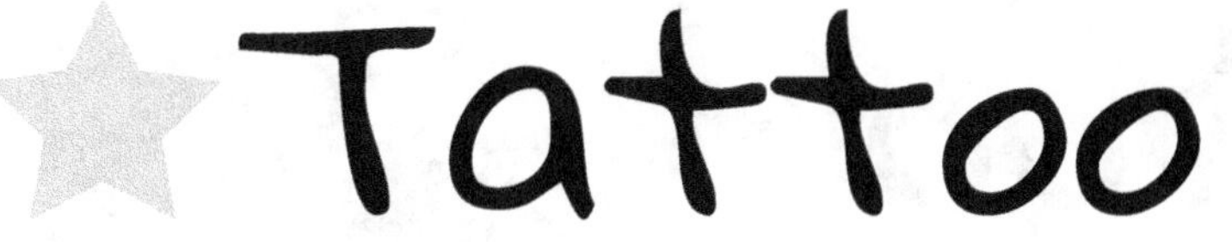 Tattoo 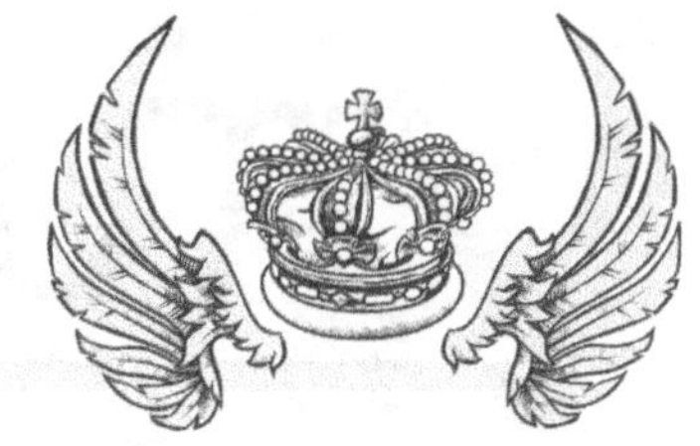

Theme ....

Placement ....

Planned Date ....

Placement

Design Palette

Suggestions

Design Idea

Detail

Notes

....

....

....

....

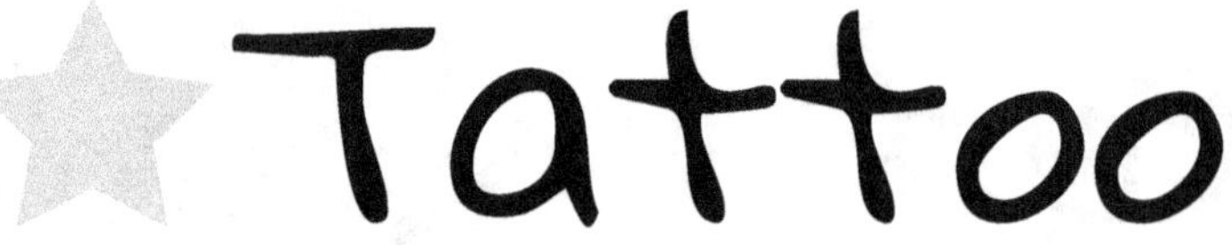 Tattoo 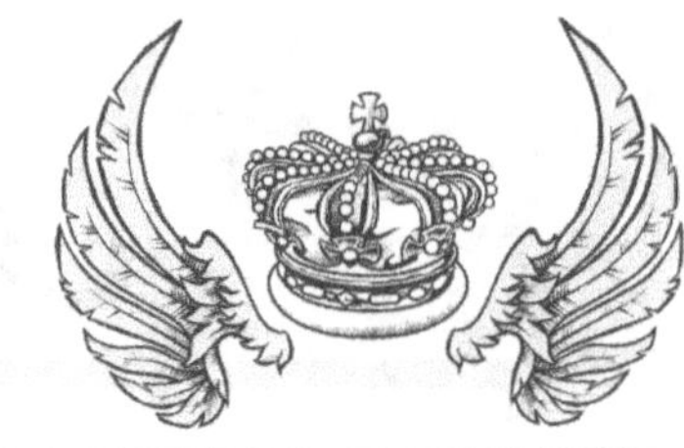

Theme ....

Placement ....

Planned Date ....

Placement

Design Palette

Suggestions

Design Idea

Detail

Notes

....

....

....

....

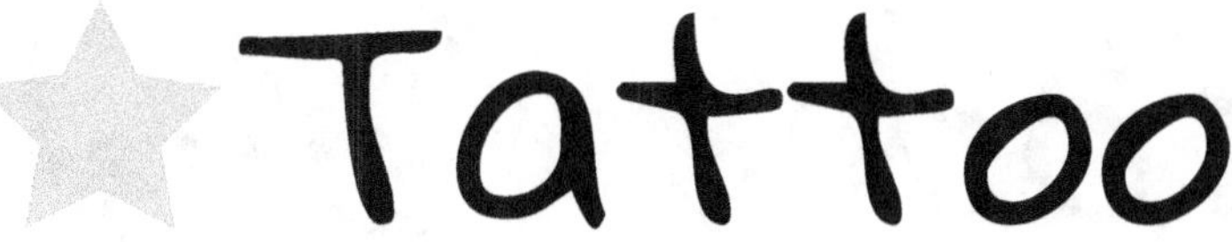 Tattoo 

Theme ....

Placement ....

Planned Date ....

Placement

Design Palette

Suggestions

Design Idea

Detail

Notes

....
....
....
....

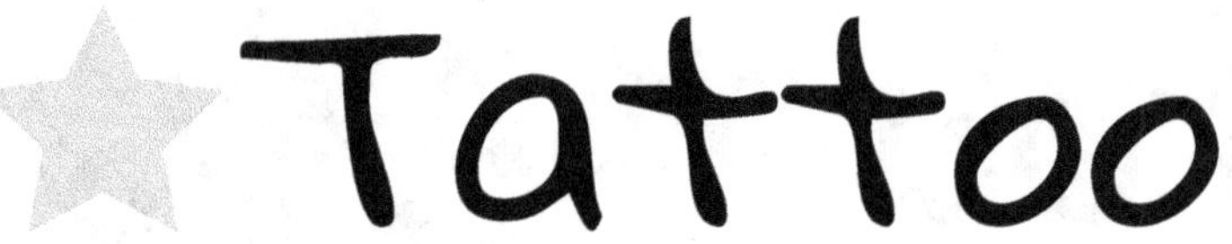 Tattoo 

Theme ....

Placement ....

Planned Date ....

Placement

Design Palette

Suggestions

Design Idea

Detail

Notes

....
....
....
....

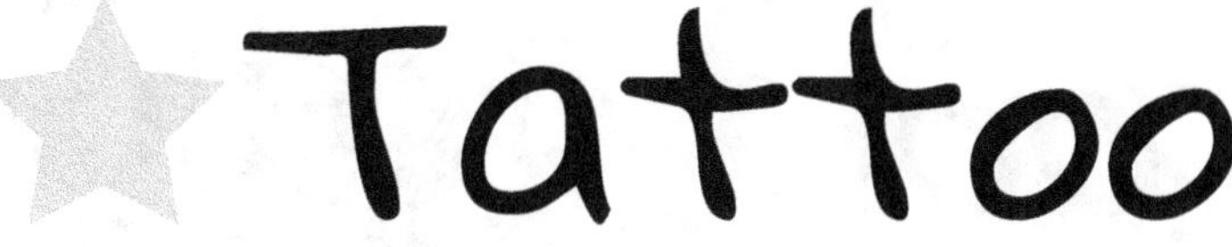 Tattoo 

Theme ....

Placement ....

Planned Date ....

Placement

Design Palette

Suggestions

Design Idea

Detail

Notes

....

....

....

....

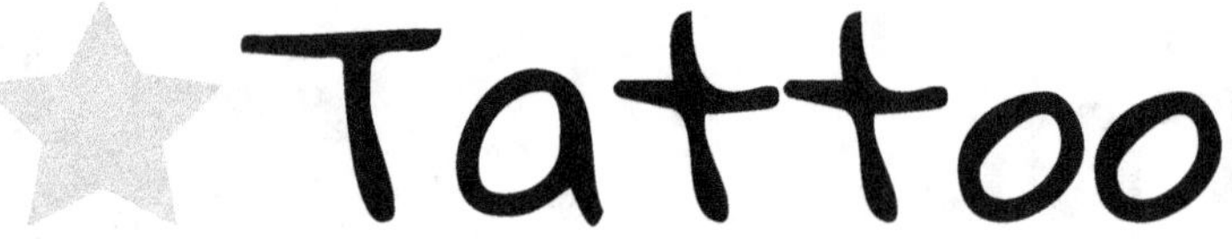 Tattoo 

Theme ....

Placement ....

Planned Date ....

Placement

Design Palette

Suggestions

Design Idea

Detail

Notes

....

....

....

....

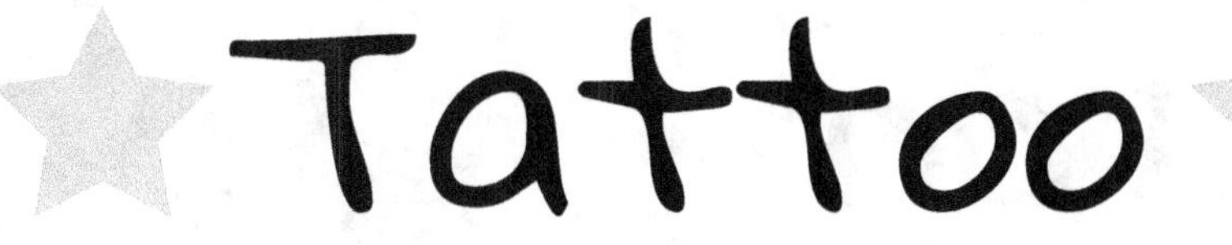 Tattoo 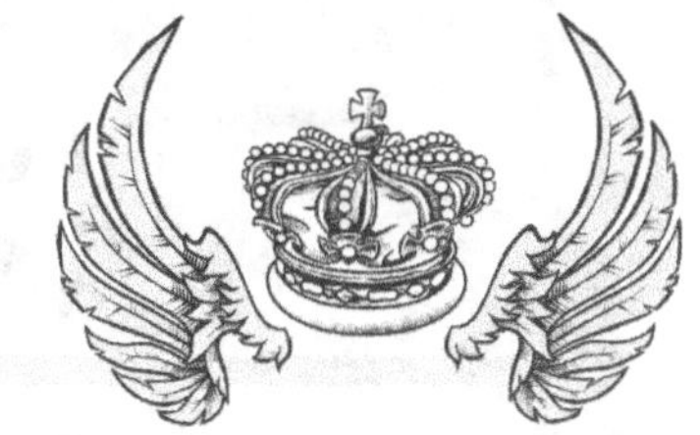

Theme ....

Placement ....

Planned Date ....

Placement

Design Palette

Suggestions

Design Idea

Detail

Notes

....

....

....

....

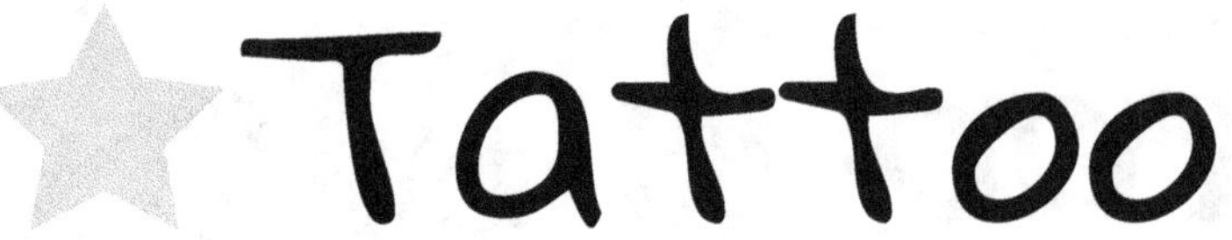 

Tattoo

Theme ....

Placement ....

Planned Date ....

Placement

Design Palette

Suggestions

Design Idea

Detail

Notes

....

....

....

....

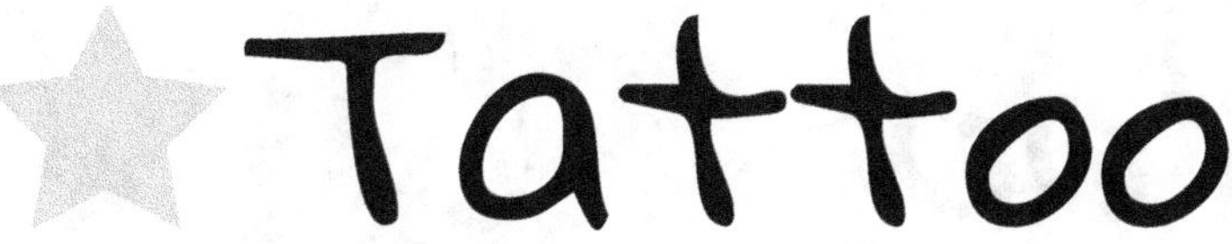 Tattoo 

Theme ....

Placement ....

Planned Date ....

Placement

Design Palette

Suggestions

Design Idea

Detail

Notes

....

....

....

....

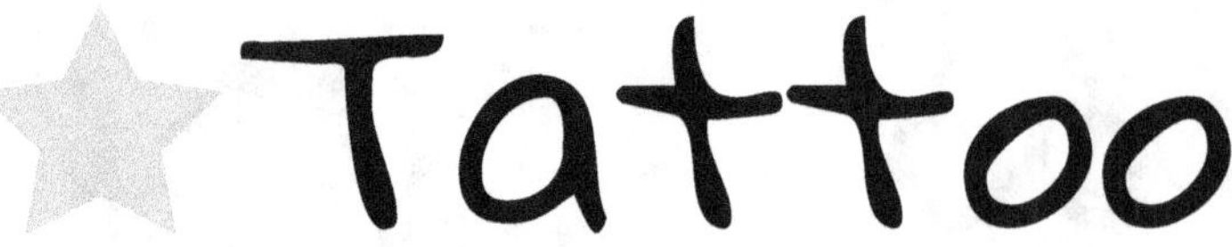 Tattoo 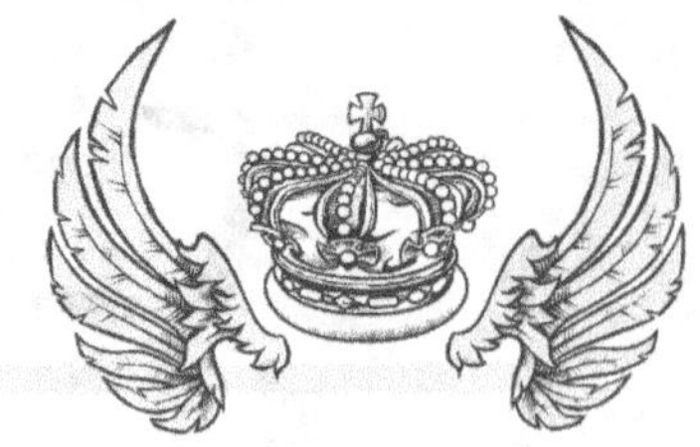

Theme ....

Placement ....

Planned Date ....

Placement

Design Palette

Suggestions

Design Idea

Detail

Notes

....

....

....

....

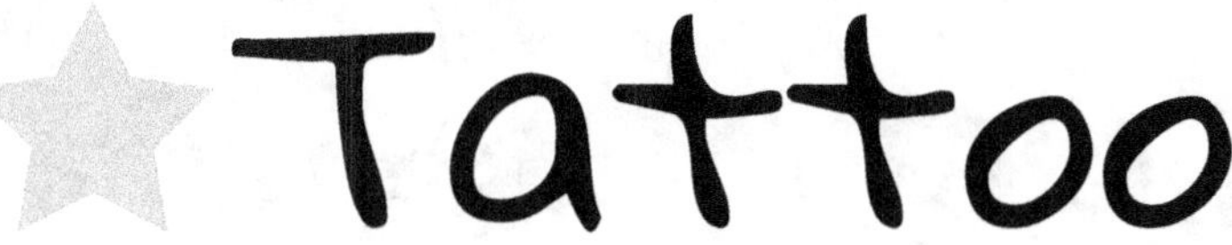 Tattoo 

Theme ....

Placement ....

Planned Date ....

Placement

Design Palette

Suggestions

Design Idea

Detail

Notes

....

....

....

....

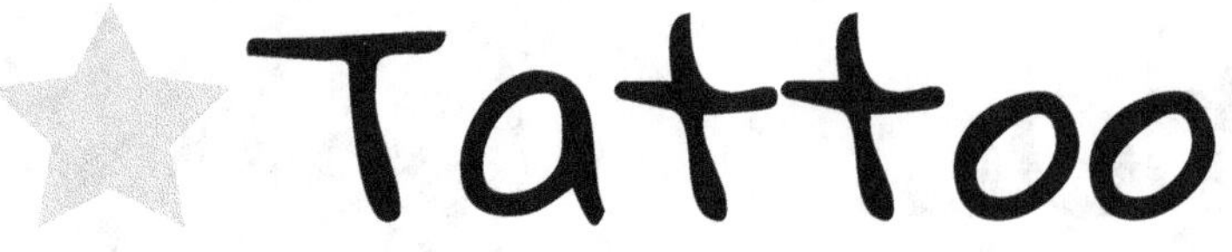 Tattoo 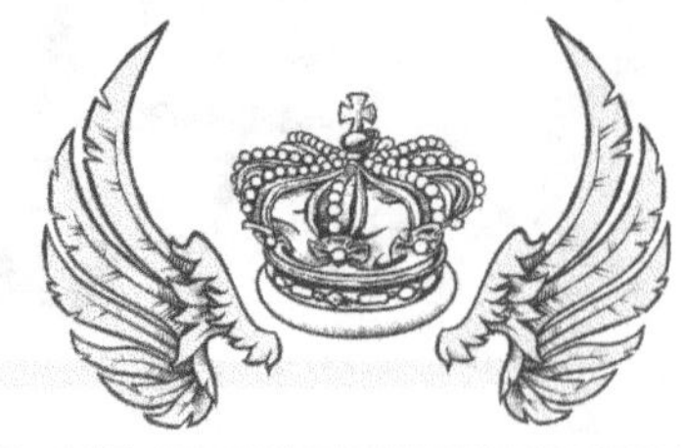

Theme ....

Placement ....

Planned Date ....

Placement

Design Palette

Suggestions

Design Idea

Detail

Notes

....

....

....

....

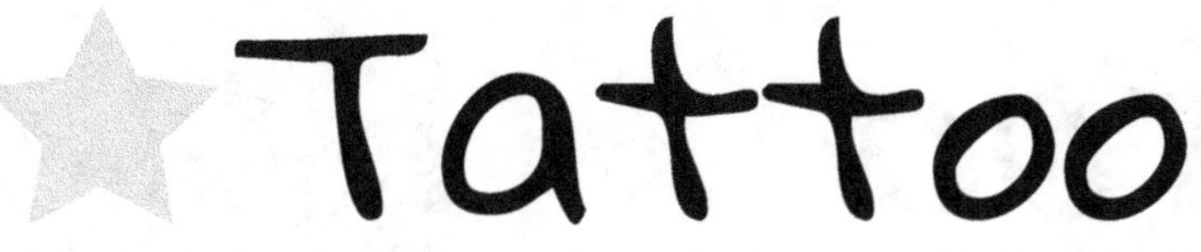 Tattoo 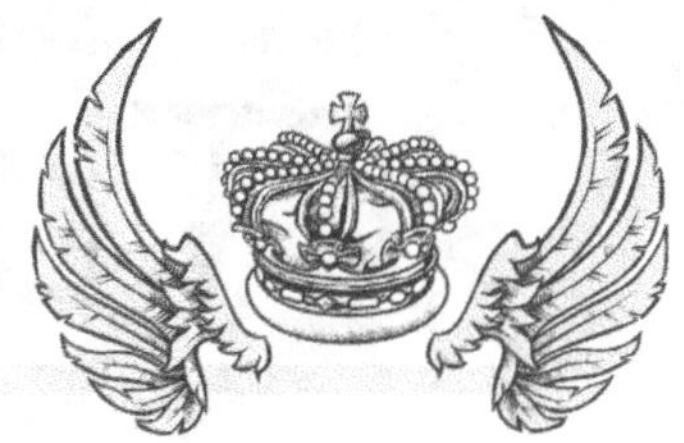

Theme ....

Placement ....

Planned Date ....

Placement

Design Palette

Suggestions

Design Idea

Detail

Notes

....

....

....

....

Tattoo

Theme ....

Placement ....

Planned Date ....

Placement

Design Palette

Suggestions

Design Idea

Detail

Notes

....

....

....

....

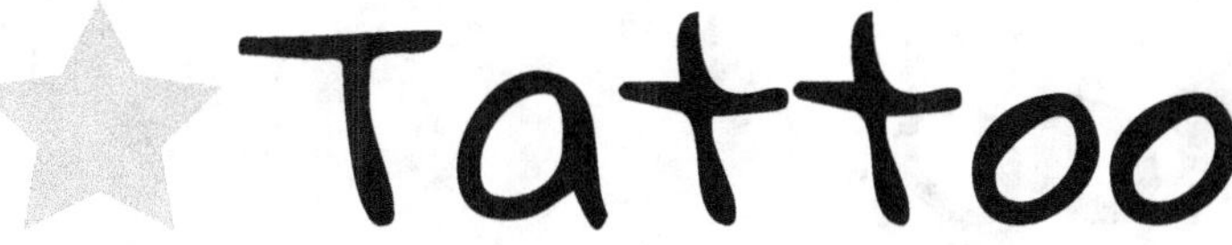 

Tattoo

Theme ....

Placement ....

Planned Date ....

Placement

Design Palette

Suggestions

Design Idea

Detail

Notes

....
....
....
....

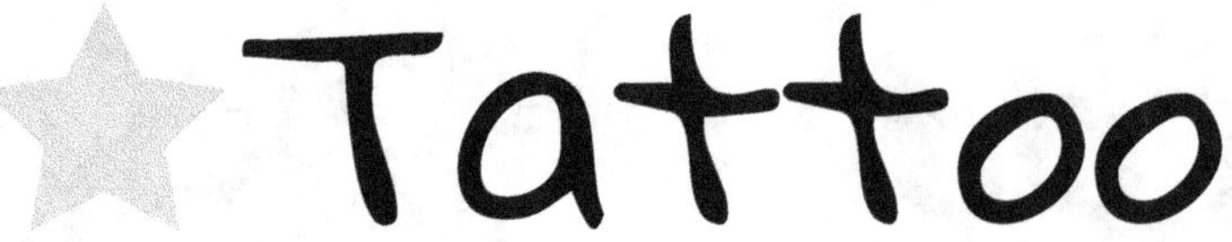 Tattoo 

Theme ....

Placement ....

Planned Date ....

Placement

Design Palette

Suggestions

Design Idea

Detail

Notes

....

....

....

....

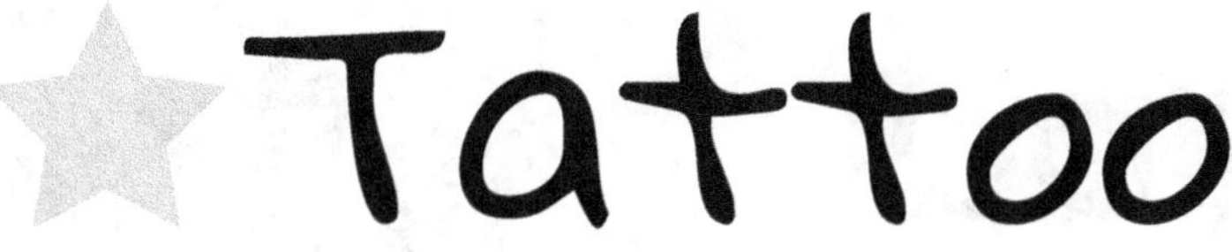 Tattoo 

Theme ....

Placement ....

Planned Date ....

Placement

Design Palette

Suggestions

Design Idea

Detail

Notes

....

....

....

....

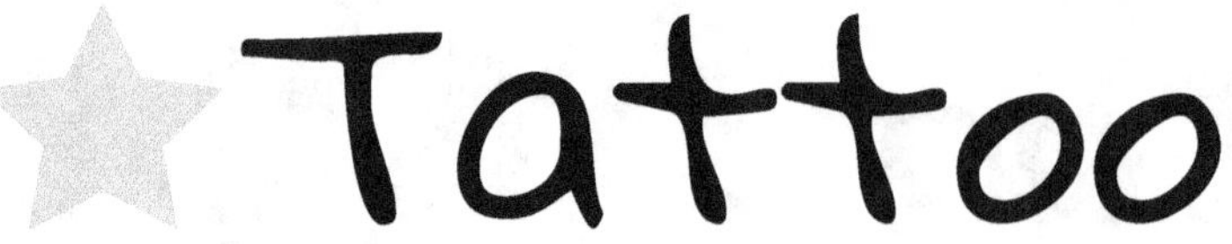 Tattoo 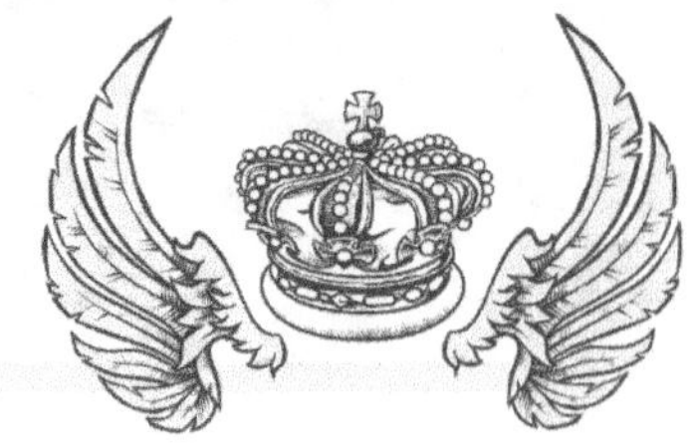

Theme ....

Placement ....

Planned Date ....

Placement

Design Palette

Suggestions

Design Idea

Detail

Notes

....
....
....
....

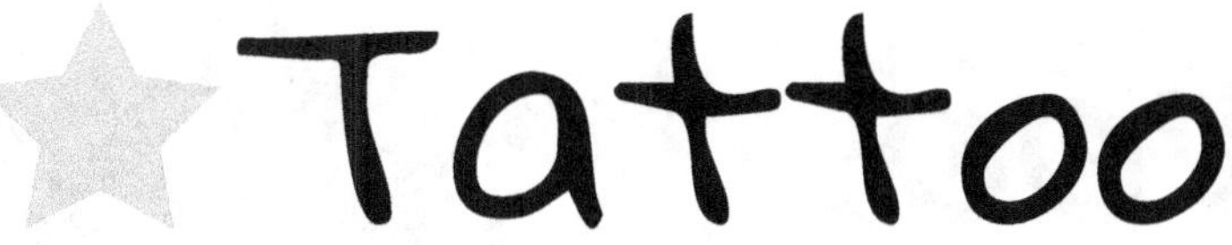 Tattoo 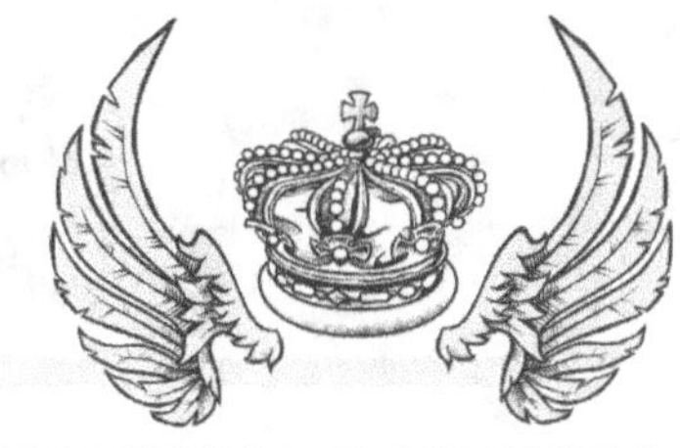

Theme ....

Placement ....

Planned Date ....

Placement

Design Palette

Suggestions

Design Idea

Detail

Notes

....

....

....

....

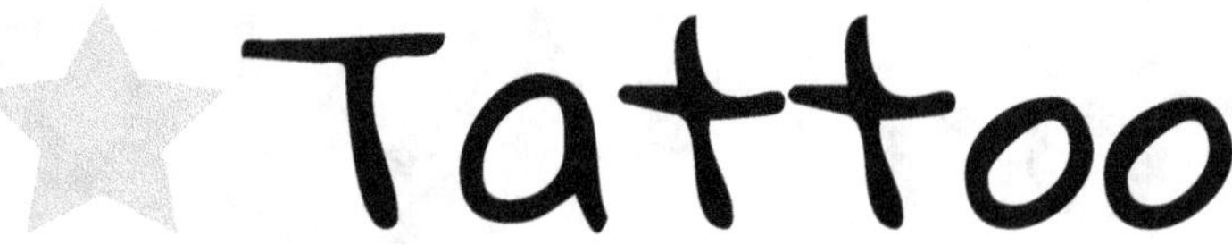 Tattoo 

Theme ....

Placement ....

Planned Date ....

Placement

Design Palette

Suggestions

Design Idea

Detail

Notes

....

....

....

....

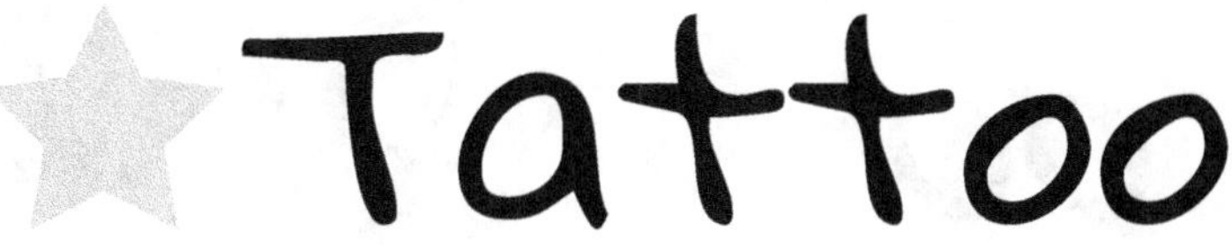 

Tattoo

Theme ....

Placement ....

Planned Date ....

Placement

Design Palette

Suggestions

Design Idea

Detail

Notes

....

....

....

....

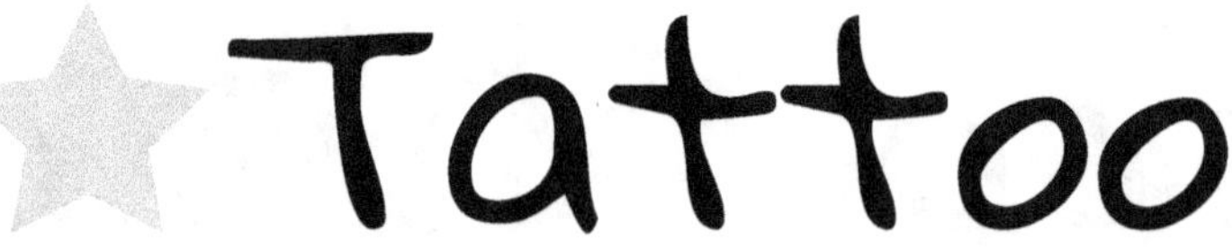Tattoo 

Theme ....

Placement ....

Planned Date ....

Placement

Design Palette

Suggestions

Design Idea

Detail

Notes

....

....

....

....

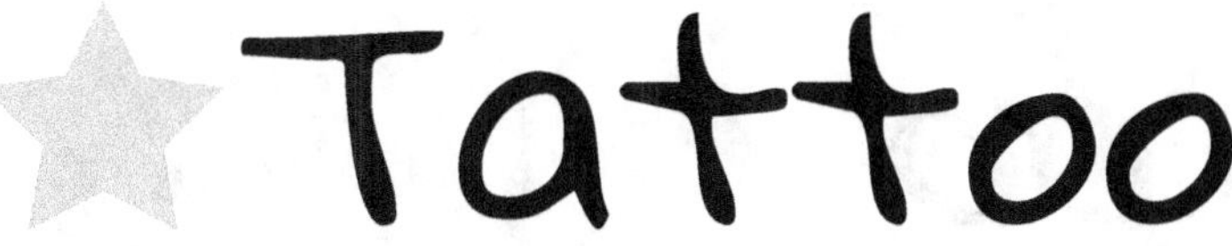 Tattoo 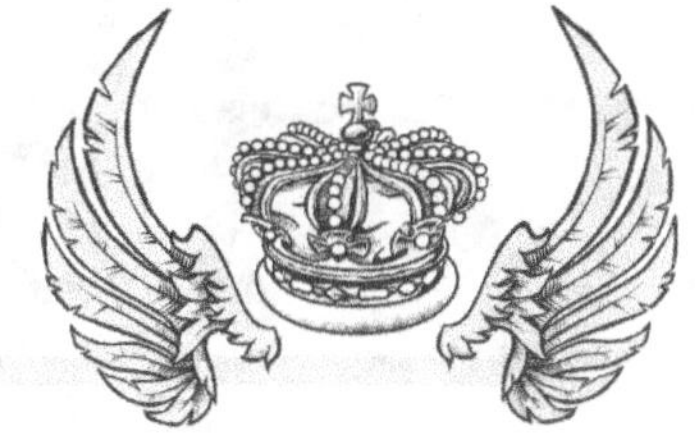

Theme ....

Placement ....

Planned Date ....

Placement

Design Palette

Suggestions

Design Idea

Detail

Notes

....

....

....

....

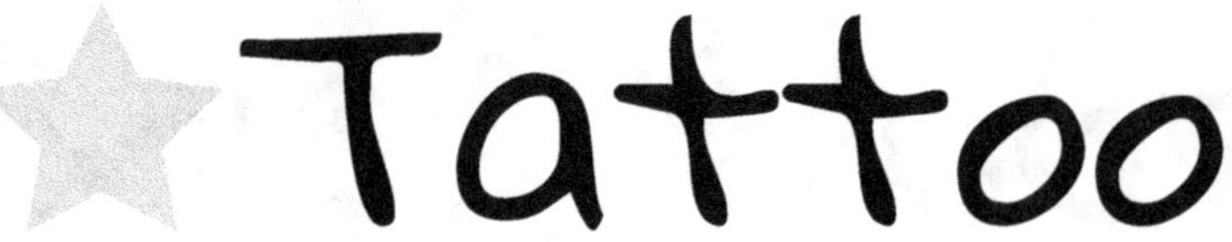 Tattoo 

Theme ....

Placement ....

Planned Date ....

Placement

Design Palette

Suggestions

Design Idea

Detail

Notes

....

....

....

....

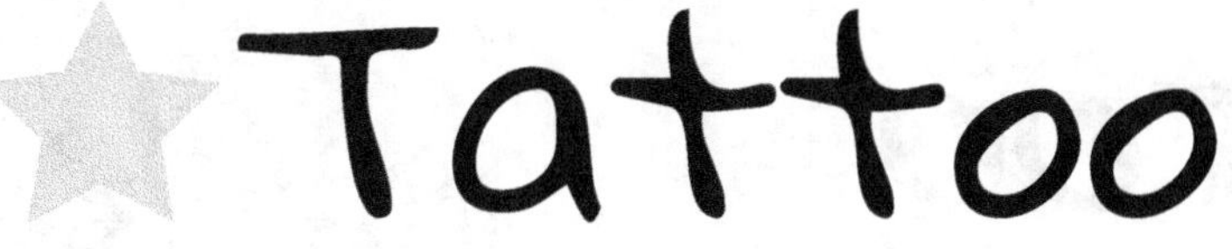 

Tattoo

Theme ....

Placement ....

Planned Date ....

Placement

Design Palette

Suggestions

Design Idea

Detail

Notes

....

....

....

....

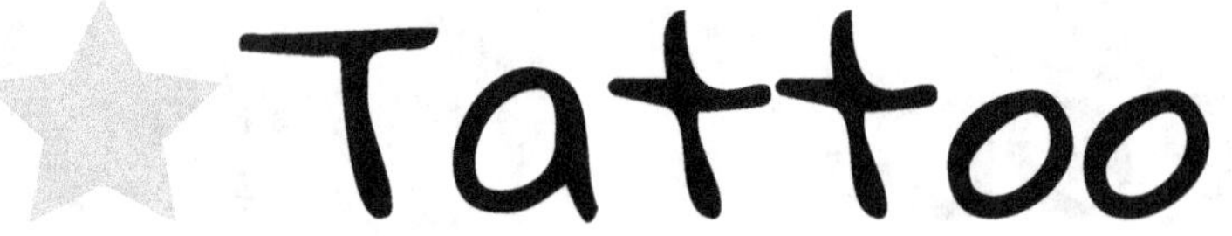 Tattoo 

Theme ....

Placement ....

Planned Date ....

Placement

Design Palette

Suggestions

Design Idea

Detail

Notes

....
....
....
....

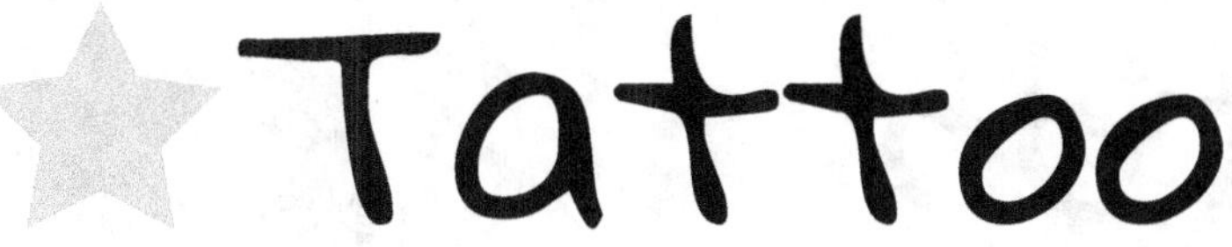 Tattoo 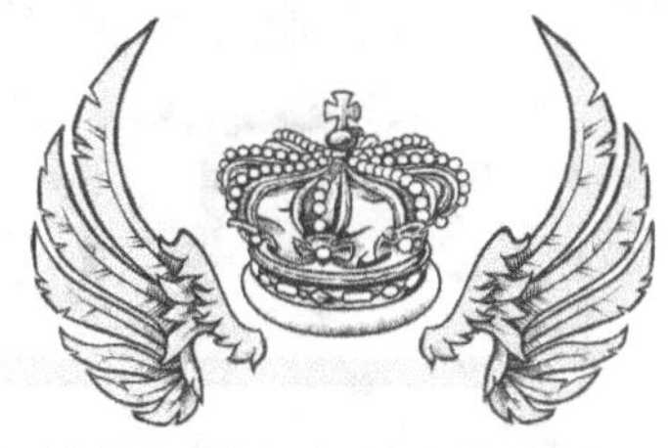

Theme ....

Placement ....

Planned Date ....

Placement

Design Palette

Suggestions

Design Idea

Detail

Notes

....
....
....
....

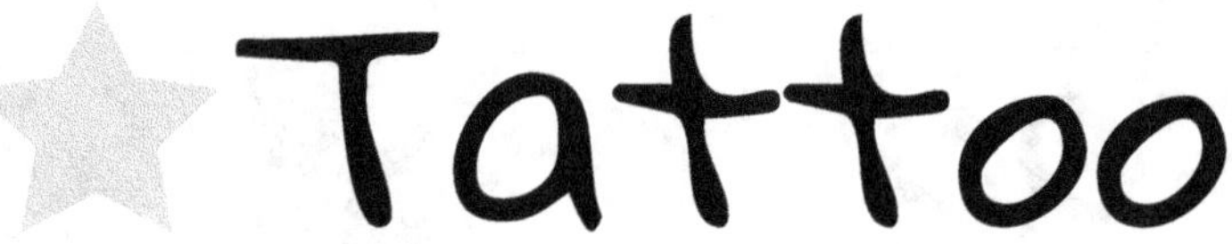 Tattoo 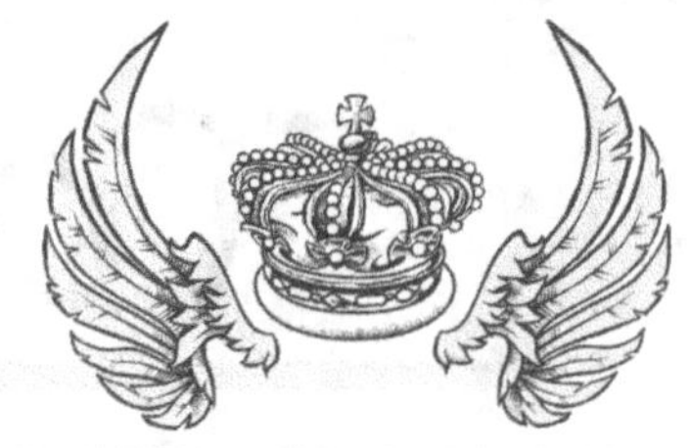

Theme ....

Placement ....

Planned Date ....

Placement

Design Palette

Suggestions

Design Idea

Detail

Notes

....
....
....
....

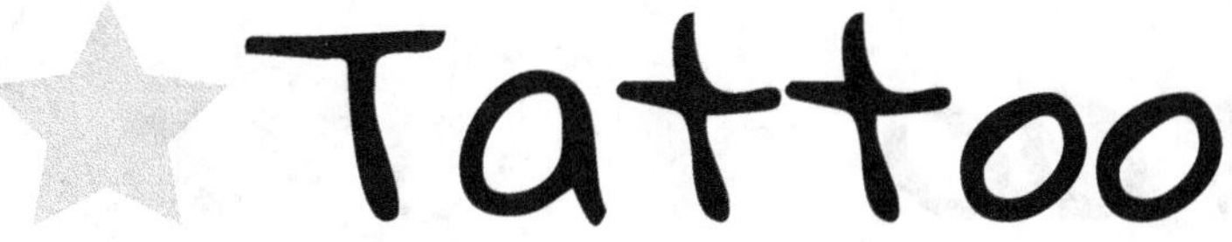 Tattoo 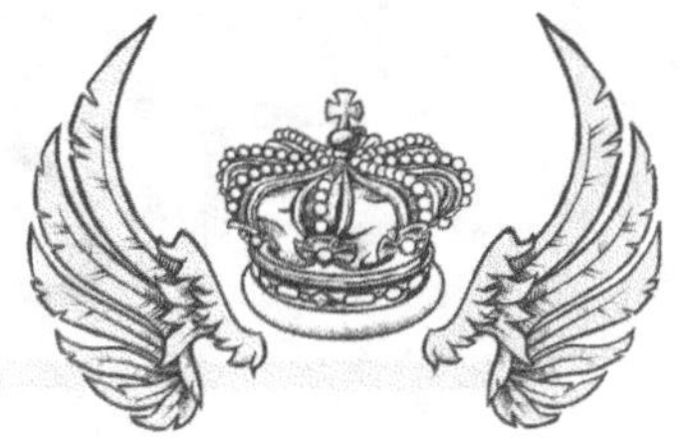

Theme ....

Placement ....

Planned Date ....

Placement

Design Palette

Suggestions

Design Idea

Detail

Notes

....
....
....
....

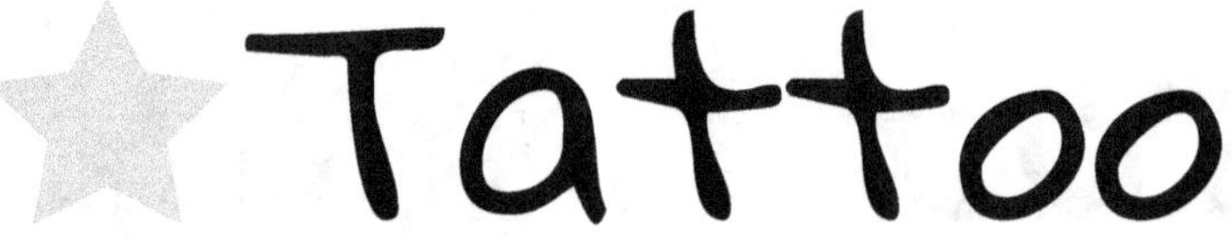 Tattoo 

Theme ....

Placement ....

Planned Date ....

Placement

Design Palette

Suggestions

Design Idea

Detail

Notes

....

....

....

....

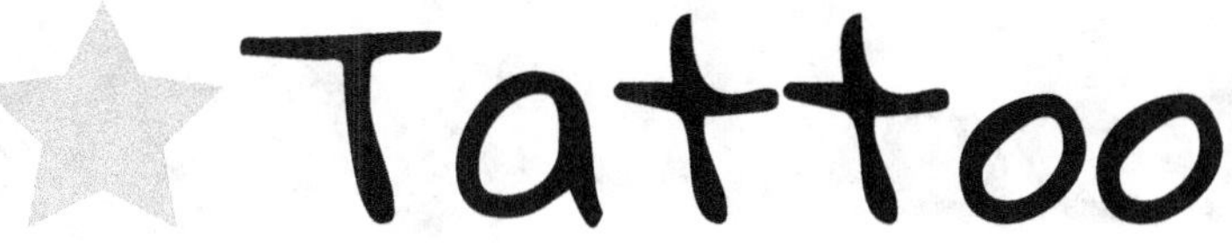 Tattoo 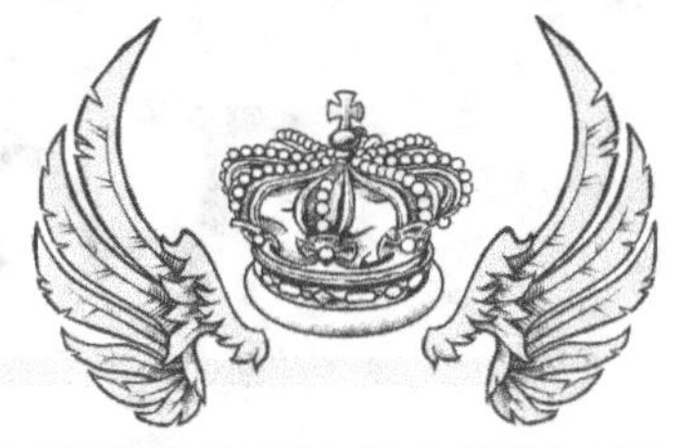

Theme ....

Placement ....

Planned Date ....

Placement

Design Palette

Suggestions

Design Idea

Detail

Notes

....

....

....

....

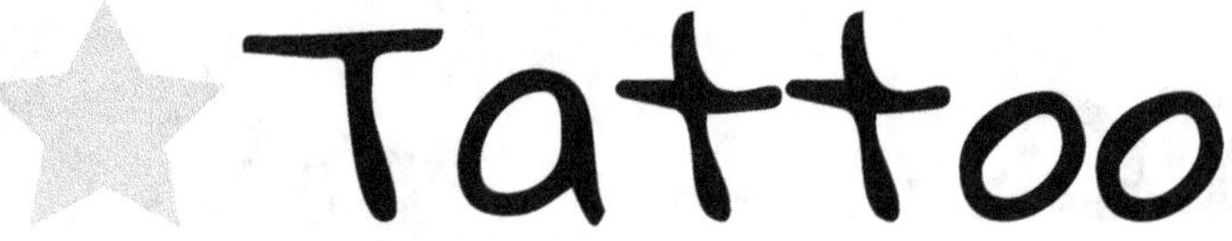 Tattoo 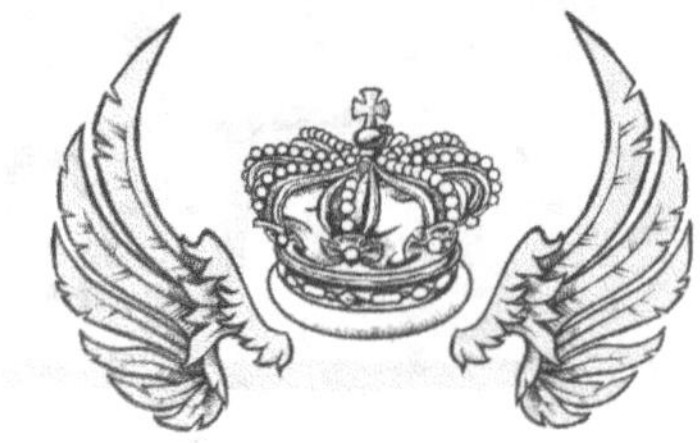

Theme ....

Placement ....

Planned Date ....

Placement

Design Palette

Suggestions

Design Idea

Detail

Notes

....

....

....

....

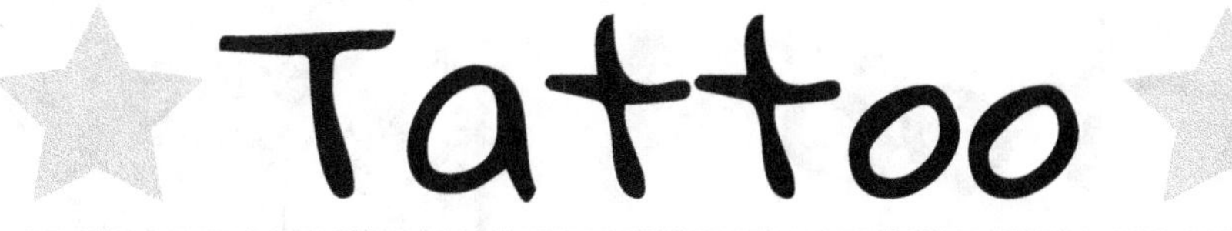Tattoo 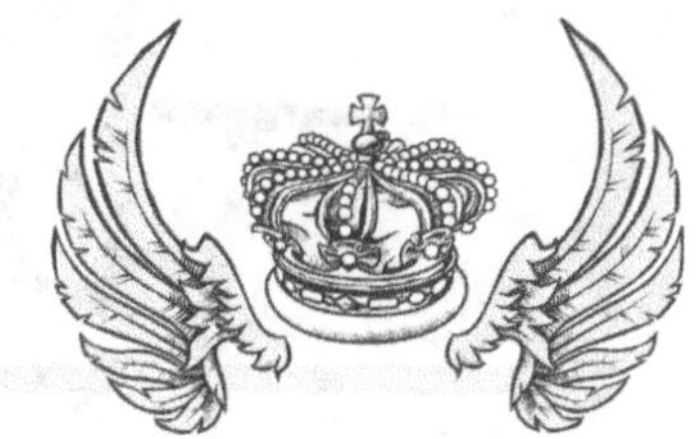

Theme ....

Placement ....

Planned Date ....

Placement

Design Palette

Suggestions

Design Idea

Detail

Notes

....

....

....

....

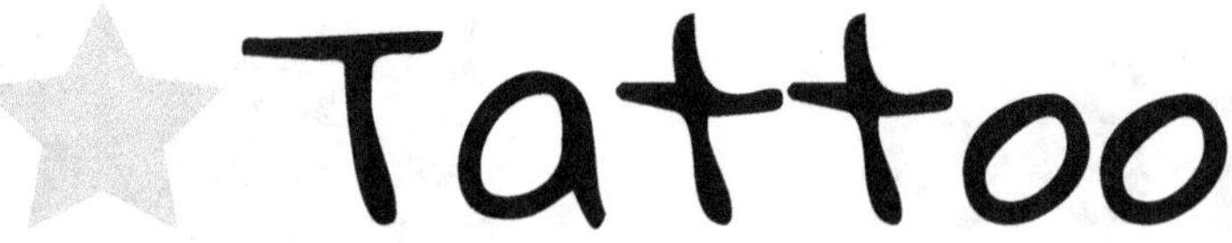 Tattoo 

Theme ....

Placement ....

Planned Date ....

Placement

Design Palette

Suggestions

Design Idea

Detail

Notes

....

....

....

....

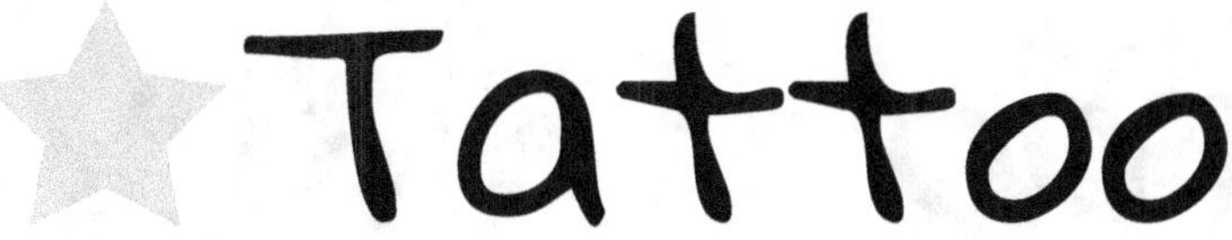 

Tattoo

Theme ....

Placement ....

Planned Date ....

Placement

Design Palette

Suggestions

Design Idea

Detail

Notes

....

....

....

....

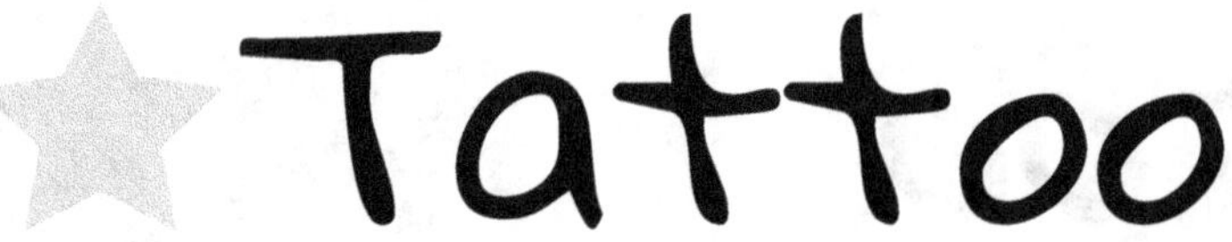 Tattoo 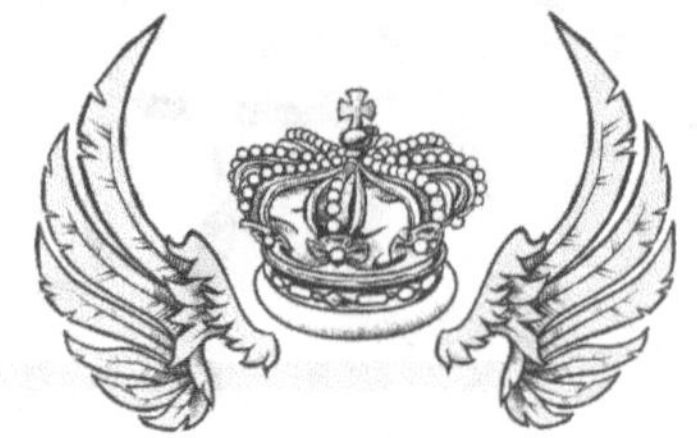

Theme ....

Placement ....

Planned Date ....

Placement

Design Palette

Suggestions

Design Idea

Detail

Notes

....

....

....

....

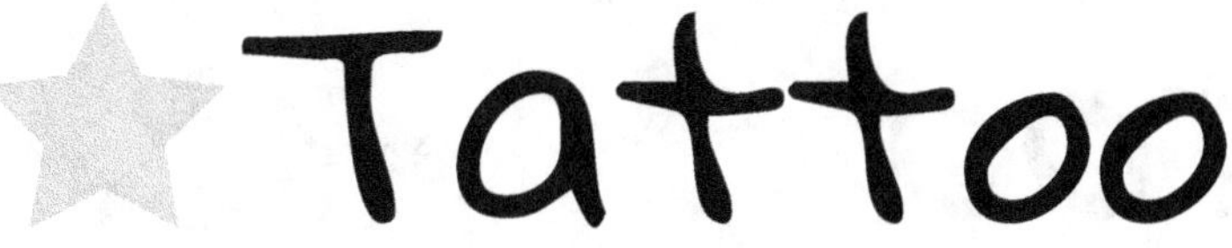 Tattoo 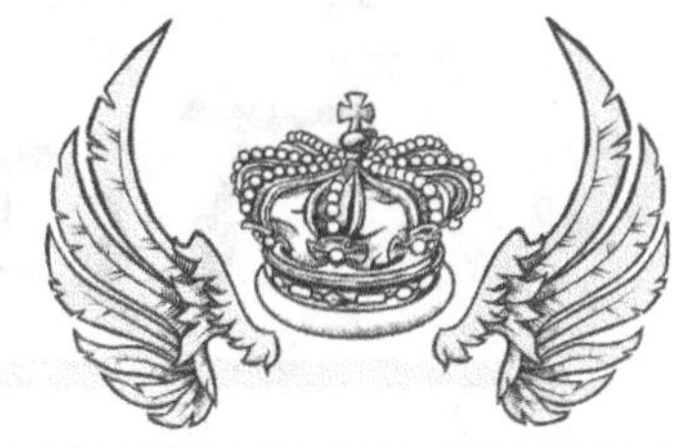

Theme ....

Placement ....

Planned Date ....

Placement

Design Palette

Suggestions

Design Idea

Detail

Notes

....

....

....

....

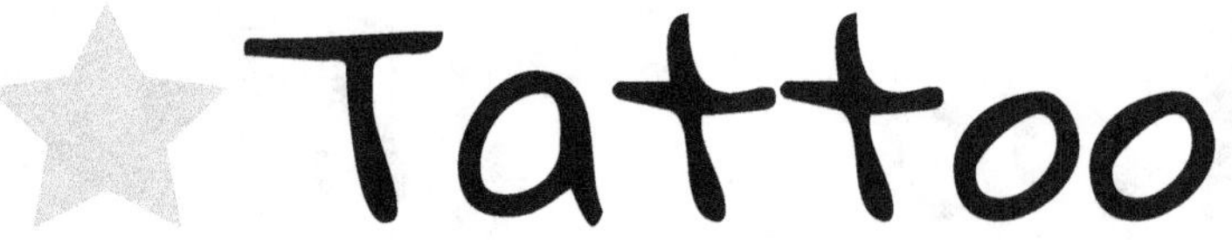 Tattoo 

Theme ....

Placement ....

Planned Date ....

Placement

Design Palette

Suggestions

Design Idea

Detail

Notes

....

....

....

....

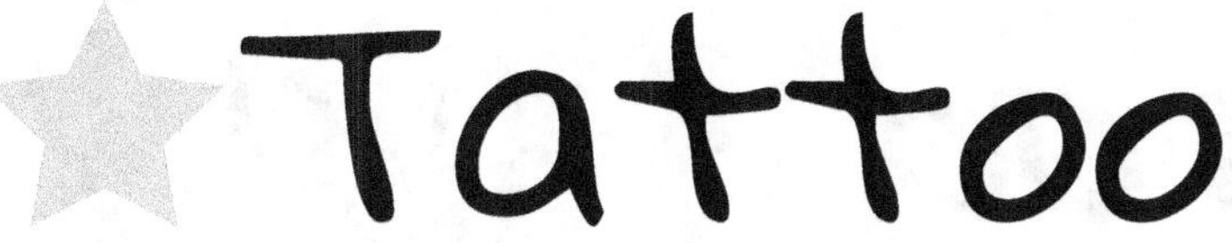

Tattoo

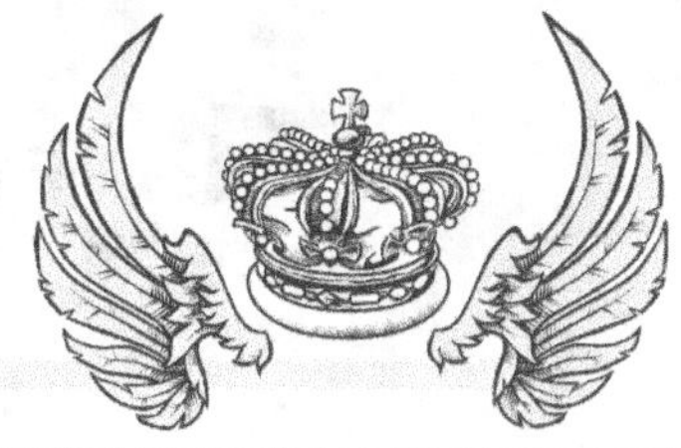

Theme ....

Placement ....

Planned Date ....

Placement

Design Palette

Suggestions

Design Idea

Detail

Notes

....

....

....

....

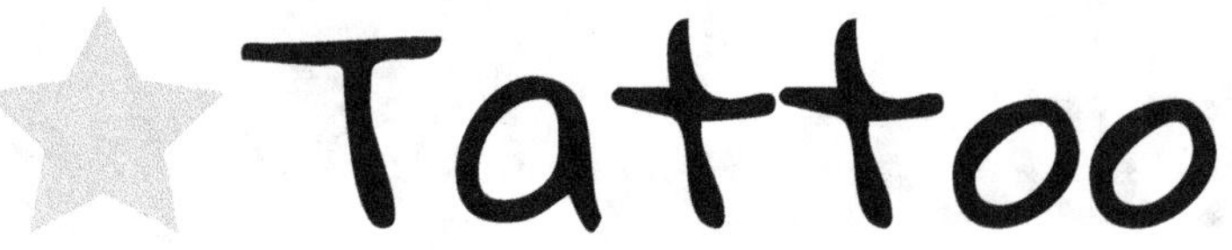 Tattoo 

Theme ....

Placement ....

Planned Date ....

Placement

Design Palette

Suggestions

Design Idea

Detail

Notes

....

....

....

....

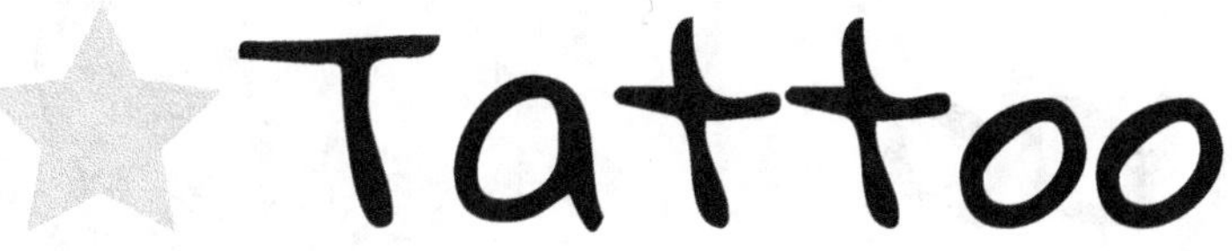 Tattoo 

Theme ....

Placement ....

Planned Date ....

Placement

Design Palette

Suggestions

Design Idea

Detail

Notes

....

....

....

....

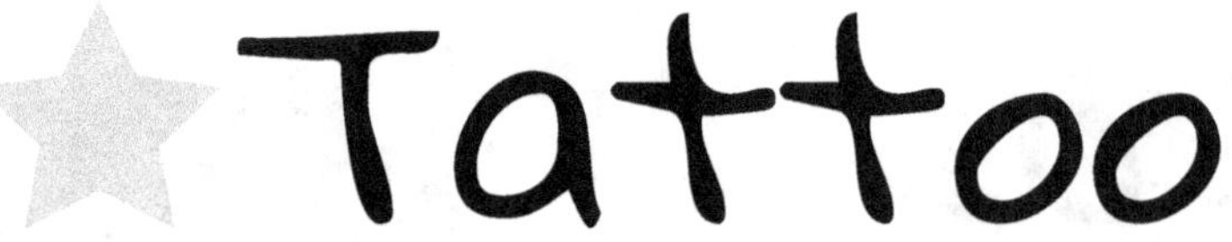

Tattoo

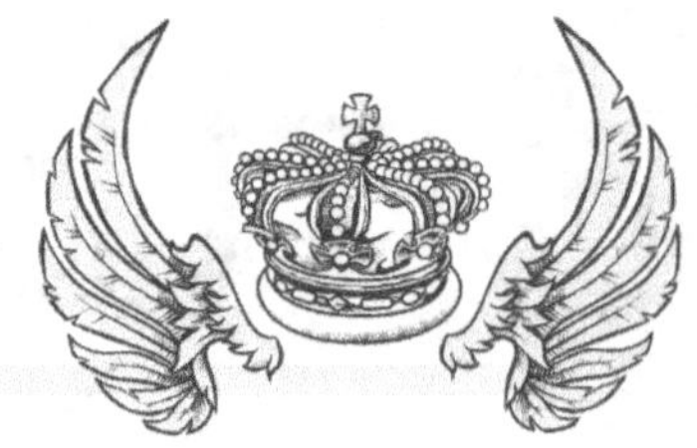

Theme ....

Placement ....

Planned Date ....

Placement

Design Palette

Suggestions

Design Idea

Detail

Notes

....
....
....
....

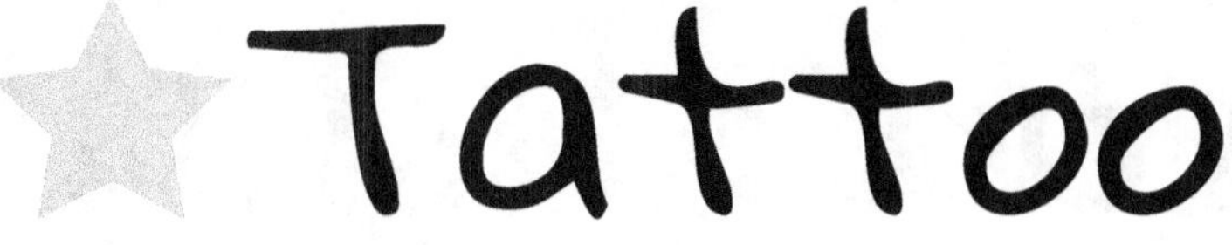 Tattoo 

Theme ....

Placement ....

Planned Date ....

Placement

Design Palette

Suggestions

Design Idea

Detail

Notes

....

....

....

....

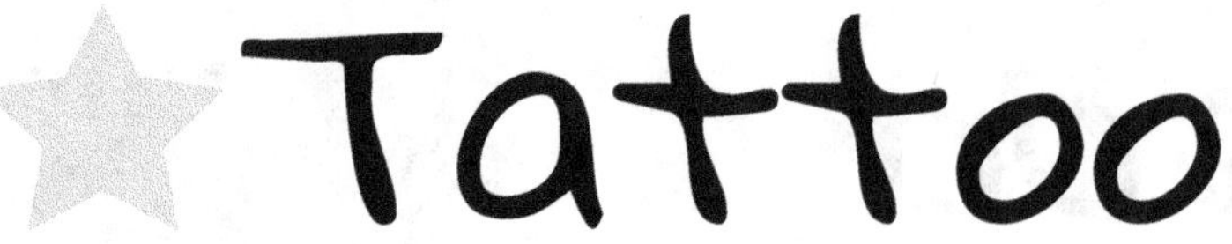 Tattoo 

Theme ....

Placement ....

Planned Date ....

Placement

Design Palette

Suggestions

Design Idea

Detail

Notes

....

....

....

....